TOD
A Man For All Reasons

An original play
by
Shaun O'Driscoll

Printed in England by Lightning Source.

ISBN 978-1-907695-19-3

Third House Publishing,
21 Laceys Lane
Exning
Newmarket
Suffolk
CB8 7HL

‘There were potential repercussions to him in revealing his past work as a professional master’

Danny Cohen, Head of Documentaries, Channel 4

‘This is ground breaking stuff’

Richard Sattin, Executive Producer *Me and My Slaves*

‘As a company we made the decision some time ago. Not to exploit or authorise the exploitation of the programme *Me and My Slaves* in any way.’

Julia Pearce, Head of Legal, Darlow Smithson Productions

‘We are returning the DVD cam 508 marked ‘Military room’. For the avoidance of doubt Channel 4 had no interest in this material’

Prash Naik, Head of Legal and Compliance, Channel 4

‘OFcom considers that Mr O’Driscoll’s compliant is not frivolous, regarding the programme *Me and My Slaves* particularly sensitive subject matter, Mr O’Driscoll’s informed consent is of a potentially serious matter.’

Janet MaClay, Case Leader, OFcom

‘Dear Mr O’Driscoll,
Without being able to prove categorically who exactly criminally damaged covert tape 508, I’m afraid we cannot proceed in this matter.’

Metropolitan Police.

Dedicated to my wife

Thank you for showing me what forgiveness is all about.

Backstory

Pimlico, London 2010

In a luxury apartment, a man's naked body is discovered stuffed into a hold-all. The circumstances of his death provide the police with a catalogue of possible explanations. However, the deceased led a controversial lifestyle that forces the investigators to confront many secret, bizarre and often dangerous sexual practices. The more they probe, the more they learn about the human psyche and the links between money, power, pain and love. All these raw emotions are surrounded by a dark cloud of addiction and compromise.

The most shocking element to emerge however is – that all this happens to be true.

Cast of Characters

John Sweeney AKA 'Tod' (deceased, not seen on stage)
A career S&M master, ex-boxer, former rent boy and deviant. *Aged 50, charismatic, violent and flawed.*

Detective Chief Inspector Jeanette Somber
Head of the investigation into Tod's death. *Early 40's, determined and focused. A 'no nonsense' woman.*

Detective Sgt Steven Miller
Vice squad veteran. *Early 50's. Male chauvinist, freemason, tough and prone to saying what he thinks no matter the effect it has on others.*

Detective Sgt Sonia Whitehead
Late 20's. High flying, ambitious feminist and deep thinker. Closet lesbian.

Detective Constable Gary Griffiths
Late 20's. Family man and conscientious worker who responds well to orders.

Paul Williams
Criminal Psychologist. L*ate 40's. 'Geeky', passionate, well-educated but also sympathetic.*

Trevor Hamilton
Home Office Coroner. *Mid 50's. Calm, collected 'seen it all before' type of man who remains unfazed.*

Richie Wenton
Professional film maker. *Late 40's/early 50's. Secretive, sly, voyeuristic. Prone to breaking rules.*

Sir James Gilfroy
Ex-government minister. *Late 60's. Freemason, millionaire business man. Powerful, well-connected, arrogant and ruthless.*

Detective Chief Superintendent George Frankish (not seen on stage)
Head of Serious Crimes and Homicide, Scotland Yard. *60's. Freemason and golf partner of Sir James Gilfroy.*

Gwen Mulvey (deceased, not seen on stage)
65, ex high class 'tart'. A psycho-sexual therapist, Christian, friend and therapist to Tod.

Gavin Mulvey
Gwen's son. *Early 30s. Former student, quiet, reflective and nursing a reservoir of anger which contrasts his humble demeanor.*

Father Declan O'Grady
Mid 30's. The warm, funny, engaging, funny and very unconventional priest of Gwen's church.

Gregory
Butler to Sir James. *Late 50's. Impeccably dressed and snobbish to the point of campness. Walks as if he's the victim of an S&M practice gone horribly wrong which left a broom handle permanently lodged in his rectum. Resembles Parker from* ***Thunderbirds****.*

Act One

Scene One

A single spotlight focuses onto a large red hold-all in the middle of the stage. A phone rings and the answering machine picks up with two beeps.

Gwen *(offstage)*
"Hello you're through to Gwen. I'm not available at the present moment, but please leave a message or a number after you hear the tone."

SFX: Bleep is heard again

Tod *(offstage)*
Gwen Baby, you must be deep in noddy land! Those friggin' tranquilizers do the business don't they?! Like a bit of night nurse myself, know what I mean? I'm having a sleepless night, so I have been reading my bible, like the good Christian boy you made me. What do you think of Proverbs Chapter 10? "A good and honest life is a blessed memorial; a wicked life leaves a rotten stench". Well my angel, you are the blessed; I guess that makes me the putrid stiff. Sleep tight; don't let the bed bugs bite.

SFX: Puts receiver down.

Sirens blaring, blue lights flashing, police radios are heard. Main lights come up to reveal the hold-all lies in the middle of a room. This has been kitted out as a torture chamber, consisting of whipping frame: vaulting horse, chains, ropes, whips, tawses, masks, rubber gear, uniforms, and hoods.

To one side sits a large gothic chair, at the side of which is a small fridge. Around the room are large black and white photos of a man in uniform. At one end is a large portrait of the same individual in a headmasters outfit, cane in hand. Boxing gloves sit in a frame surrounded by more photographs. Underneath the red hold-all a small pool of liquid is seen. The area has been taped off as a crime scene and a uniformed ***policeman*** *stands guard at the perimeter.*

Two ***people*** *dressed in white contamination suits (Scene of crime officers = 'Soco's') carrying bags flash their IDs, passing through the tape to begin the investigation. Shortly afterwards a* ***man*** *in a blue contamination suit makes his way over to the bag. One starts to take photographs while the other two begin their examination. Next three suited* ***detectives****, two* ***female****, one* ***male****, put on* *overshoes, masks, and gloves and having shown the* ***constable*** *their warrant cards, make their way around the room. All congregate round the hold-all.*

Jeanette *(to Soco1)*
DCI Jeanette Somber of Scotland Yard homicide and serious crime command. This is DS Sonia Whitehead, over there is DC Gary Griffiths. Okay what we got, aside from a nasty stench in a kinky den?

Soco 1
We have a nude male, badly decomposed. The bag was padlocked from the outside, which we have removed for forensic examination. It was a travel style lock, and was pushed through the two zip fasteners. The heating was turned to full, even though it's the middle of August. However the windows are all open, probably to ventilate the flat, and buy time. Lights were all turned off and the front door was double locked from the outside. We've yet to locate any keys.

Jeanette
I see the coroner is already hard at it.

Trevor
And a good morning to you too, Jeanette.

Jeanette
Trevor – I'll get to you in a moment. *(To Gary)* Gary do me a favor. Call Detective Sgt Steve Miller over at vice. Given the nature of the surroundings, I'd appreciate his insight. Also, get hold of Paul Williams – criminal psychologist. Tell him we have a juicy case for his weird shit file. He'll understand the implications.

Gary
Will do, ma'am.

Sonia *(to Soco2)*
Who made the initial call to the police?

Soco 2
The constable who signed you in was the first on the scene, sarge. He has a witness statement for you.

Sonia
Good. Shall we find out the circumstances and give the coroner more time?

Jeanette
Might be an idea. Trevor doesn't like to be rushed.

Sonia and Jeanette cross to the uniformed PC

Sonia

So, mind telling us just who reported what, constable?

Constable

I was on foot patrol two streets away when I got a call to attend a suspicious smell reported by the letting agent. She had requested assistance in entering a locked property, which they had a spare key for. On arrival, the agent informed me that a neighbor a Mr. Peter Corney had rang him to alert him to an awful stench that was getting worse by the hour. Both had identified this dwelling as the source of the smell. They tried knocking – no answer. The tenant living here is a John Sweeney who has not been seen for at least a week. I told them to wait outside and let myself in with the spare key. All the lights were turned off, but I immediately noticed the hold-all in the centre of the room – that's where the smell was coming from. You get to recognise the smell of decaying flesh. The bag was locked but I could feel the outline of the body.

Sonia

You used gloves?

Constable

Yes, ma'am. Like I said – I know the procedure. I searched the rest of the premises then sealed the crime scene before calling it in. While I was waiting I took statements from both the agent and Mr. Corney.

Sonia

And what did Mr Corney have to say about his neighbor, John Sweeney?

Constable

Just that he had complained about the constant noise from Mr. Sweeney's flat about a month ago.

Sonia

What sort of noise?

Constable

Shouting, screaming, sometimes crying, and even laughter. He went round and knocked the door, only to be greeted door by a sweating and out of breath Mr. Sweeney who was dressed head to toe in leather; peaked hat pulled firmly down. In his words, 'looking like a devil possessed'.

Sonia

And how did Mr. Sweeney react to the complaint?

Constable *(coughs)*

I have it here ma'am. *(Reads statement)* 'My dear boy, can't you see I'm busy doing my fucking housework?! Now be a good lad and run along. Otherwise I will be compelled to break your handsome jaw in three different places. Ciao.' According to Mr. Corney the door was then slammed shut and he retreated.

Jeanette

So, the neighbor from hell or what?!

Constable

Here's the post script. The next day Mr. Corney received a delivery of a very large bunch of lilies and a magnum of champagne, attached to which a card which read: 'Sorry for the outburst, very uncivilized of me. I will keep the hoovering to a minimum in the future. Warm regards, Tod.'

Jeanette

Tod must be a nickname. Well, at least he had a sense of humour, as well as a sense of guilt. This man is either black or white, but not grey in-between.

Trevor

Well he's 50 shades of green at the gills now.

The detectives cross to where Trevor is examining the body in the hold-all.

Jeanette

So, what we got Trevor?

Trevor

One naked Caucasian male. Aged between thirty five and fifty five. Badly decomposed, and lying on his back with his legs pulled up to his chest in a fetal position. No obvious sign of injuries, except some bruising on the elbows. This could be due to either being restrained or lifted. I'm afraid the state of the rest of the cadaver makes it nigh on impossible to find bruising in other areas. I might find out better at the morgue. There are no fractures or broken bones that I can determine. No defense wounds on his hands, which were across his chest in almost in a praying posture. No signs of trauma or any indications of him trying to escape the confines of the bag. He almost looks at peace. Large amount of lividity gathered in the groin area, which would be expected as his legs are pulled up. The putrefaction has penetrated the plastic bag and gathered underneath. There appears to be an excess amount of liquid that I normally wouldn't expect to find. It could be that water was thrown over the body whilst he was lying in the bag.

Sonia

Could someone have been trying to eliminate DNA by washing it off his body?

Trevor

Possibly.

Jeanette

Well, by the surroundings and the *er* – interior decoration, I think it would be fair to say the person who lived here had more than a passing interest in the bizarre and quite frankly, the unnatural. Is it possible he got into the bag of his own violation with the intention of performing some sort of self-sexual practice?

Trevor

It's certainly worth pursuing. *(to the Soco's)* Can we turn him over officers, please?

The two Soco's help the coroner turn the body still in the bag.

Trevor

Well I'll be damned.

Jeanette

What?

Trevor

The keys to the padlock were lying underneath his torso.

Sonia

So – was he doing something sexual and intended to somehow unlock the bag from the inside and exit it at some point after?

Jeanette

We can have the hold-all examined by the national policing improvement agency. They have officers who specialize in survival in confined spaces.

Sonia

I'll get hold of the Houdini squad straight away. We should establish if the hold-all actually belongs to the victim.

Gary

Sorry to interrupt. Steve from vice is here, ma'am.

DS Miller dons a mask, gloves, and overshoes, shows his warrant card to the PC.

Jeanette

Steve, thanks for coming so soon. How are you?

Steve *(looking up at the portrait)*

I'm overworked, overtaxed, overweight, and now over here. I see you have found our Master Tod. Or is it another one of his punters?

Jeanette

So you know who this is?

Steve *(peering into hold-all)*

Right now I'm looking at something that resembles a gherkin with a set of teeth. But if that's my man Sweeney then I'm not surprised. (*Pointing at photos)* I've been onto Tod's arse for well over 25 years now. We go back a long way.

Sonia

The named occupier is one John Sweeney.

Steve

John Sweeney, nicknamed 'Tod' as in Sweeney Tod.

Jeanette

So what can you tell us about him?

Steve

What can't I tell you about this monster? He goes way back to the early 80's when he started selling his backside off the meat rack at Piccadilly Circus. Picked up numerous times and given warnings for importuning but never charged. He quickly diversified into providing the sort of extreme and dangerous services most hustlers won't entertain. Quickly moved up this food chain of bottom-feeders with a rep for hardcore sado masochistic scenes. Next he puts together his own stable of well-healed clients, gets paid top dollar and ends up buying a property in the East end complete with dungeons, classrooms, torture chambers – even a medical procedures lab. He called himself 'Master Mengele' after the Nazi concentration camp doctor.

Sonia

Just your average nice respectable neighbourhood sadist.

Steve

Then in 1981, he was linked to the Commander Trestrail scandal.

Jeanette

The what?

Steve

Michael Trestrail – the Queens personal bodyguard. *The News of the World* exposed his long-term relationship with a rent boy called Rauche. Had to resign his post and then faded into obscurity. But it wasn't Rauche who sold the story to the paper for £10,000. Rauche had confided in Tod about his 'special' police client. He wanted Tod to perform a particularly strong sexual practice on Trestrail that he couldn't do himself. Tod was a ruthless opportunist. When he was 19 he'd been involved in a gun siege in Coventry. He wouldn't hesitate in destroying the career of a police officer who he regarded with distain.

Jeanette

Gun siege?

Steve

Yes, I'll bring up the details for you.

Sonia

So this Rauche kind of sub-contracted him, yes?

Steve

Sub...*(pause)*- contracted – oh very good! Dominant and subservient. Steve Miller.

Sonia

Sonia Whitehead. Sorry – that pun was purely unintentional.

Steve

Don't worry. With this type of case these little one liners come thick and fast. (*beat*) See what I mean? We've a rule in vice that whoever comes up with one puts a pound in the kitty. Then at the end of the month we all go out and get smashed with the proceeds.

Jeanette

What else can you tell us about Tod?

Steve

Apart from a propensity to exploit the pink pound? Pretty decent boxer – ABA semi finalist in fact. But he chose a very different form of violence to make his fortune. We're talking a world wide operator with close links to Italy, Holland, and Belgium. In the past, we've tried to do him for running a brothel within a sauna, pimping male prostitutes, importuning, and I think we also caught him in a cottage swoop, but he got let off with a caution.

Jeanette

Cottage being of the thatched roof variety?

Steve

No guv, more like the piss palaces of the London underground variety. He was doing a George Michael, if you know what I mean! We also linked him with the production of extremely violent porn films, some of which we were not certain as to whether they were fake snuff films, or the genuine article. Two former clients had died in suspicious circumstances. He was also involved in the infamous spanner case of 1986. At that time, he was the leather master to a Graham Cadman – an ice cream sales man dealing in porno films on the sly. In a raid at his address we found a collection of extreme S&M films, one showing a man's penis being nailed to a gate. *(Nudging Trevor)* Thought that might make your eyes water, mate.

Trevor

(exhales painfully)

Steve

Cadman then tried to buy himself out of a bit of jail time by grassing up a group of 20 or so men, who readily agreed when questioned that they had been part of an informal but clandestine posse of S&M worshippers who had done unspeakable acts of violence and humiliation on each other, sometimes filming these grotesque performances. They thought wrongly that consent meant it was lawful. Because we had gone in thinking they were doing snuff movies we were then committed into following the case all the way through to the European courts who a couple of years later upheld the view that no man or woman could in their right mind allow another person to inflict actual bodily harm to that extent of injury with consent. It was an unacceptable defense. The outcome was: six were jailed, two subsequently committed suicide, but nearly all were ruined by it. Except Teflon Tod on whom nothing seemed to stick. He just seemed to emerge stronger if anything and continued to ply his vile trade. In later interviews with vice squad officers, he always said if he could consent to some opponent trying to cause him brain damage in the boxing ring, then he felt more than comfortable administering pain and torture outside of it – and without that damage or serious injury to a paying and willing client. I guess he had a valid point there.

Jeanette

But let's be crystal clear on this, every time he beat someone with an implement, causing actual bodily harm, he was breaking the law, yes?

Steve

Oh yes and he knew it. As a direct consequence of the threat of being jailed, he decided to take up with an Italian Duke in 1990. He said if you invest in the over 65's, they give you life long loyalty. So, he spends the next 15 years providing an exclusive and very extreme servicing to this multi millionaire from Milan. He even went as far to branding his initials into his noble backside. Tod by name, sod by nature. After the Duke's death in 2005, he self-imploded and for some strange reason went and confessed everything in a film commissioned by Channel 4, "Me & My Slaves". Not long after he wrote his memoirs in a book with the same title which was the subject of legal action taken up by a disgruntled punter. Both the offending publication and then Tod disappeared from circulation. Literally.

Trevor

Excuse me Jeanette, but there's a large amount of fairly fresh blood around the whipping frame. You'll have the toxicology results tomorrow and I'll fast-track the rest.

Jeanette

Thanks, Trevor. I've got a horrible gut feeling this one is going to be sensitive for a lot of people out there who knew him. He was a pollution in life, but will be a bigger one in death, I think.

Sonia *(to Gary)*

Trace Tod's next of kin. We'll have to use his DNA and dental records to confirm who this is. I wouldn't want anyone who knew him to see him in this state. No-one deserves to end up like this, not even a monster like Tod.

Gary

Will do, Sarge

Soco 1

Ma'am, there's a small fridge here. Three bottles of good quality fizz, three strong lagers, a bag of frozen prawns, and two bottles of amyl nitrate – one opened, one unused.

Jeanette

Dust for prints. Amyl nitrate – poppers?

Soco 1

Correct. A very powerful and somewhat addictive sexual stimulant – inhaled either directly from the bottle, or put into a mask or cloth. Increases the blood flow to the heart, making it beat faster and supposedly increasing the intensity of orgasm.

Jeanette

Hmm, must get my old man some for his birthday. Can you tell if our victim partook, Trevor?

Trevor

What's left of the nostril cavity might retain some particles captured within the small hairs, but I'll have to do a microscopic inspection at the lab.

Sonia

But if he had used them at the time of death, surely they'd be in the bag with him?

Trevor

Good point. They can be very addictive, but only give a short hit. So he'd hardly leave them in the fridge if he was pleasuring himself in the bag.

Soco 2

Gives a whole new meaning to boil in the bag . . .

Steve

That one deserves a quid in the kitty.

Sonia

What about suicide? He had been around a long time, surviving highs and lows in a complicated game of give and take. He could have topped himself.

Steve

He gave, they took. I think his whole business had come to a halt after his self-outing in the film and the book. But by what we've got here, it looks as if he may have gone back to his old ways. I can't imagine people would trust him. He'd have lost his credibility as a master and to some degree, his kudos. In the film he effectively crucified himself and was even accused by the film maker of being blasphemous. They even showed a fisting scene.

Jeanette

Fisting, you mean beating up?

Steve

No, I mean – *(he demonstrates a fist movement on his own backside)*

Jeanette

Please tell me that's not on his menu of services?!

Steve

'fraid so. He was renowned for his skill of tickling colons with his fingers. He referred to this as his 'foreign objects, in foreign parts' routine.

Jeanette

Yuk! This gets grimmer by the minute.

Steve

Alimentary, my dear Watson. *(at Soco 2's look)* Yeah, that's another quid. It'll get worse as we open up his life, believe me. I'm pretty sure he was in a state of crisis so there's a high probability he's done himself in. He always said that everybody has a shelf life and that he was well past the use-by date.

***Paul Williams** enters. Dons mask and gloves, and shows his ID to the constable before entering the crime scene.*

Trevor

If it was suicide, we have to prove he was able to lock the bag from the inside as well as locking the front door from the outside. I somehow think we can't do that.

Jeanette

Fe fi fo fum, I smell the blood of a murdered son. Oh – Paul, over here. (*Shakes his hand)* Thanks for coming so soon.

Steve

That's another pound in the kitty.

Paul

Sorry?

Steve

(Holding out his hand) Doesn't matter. DS Steve Miller, nice to meet you.

Paul

Paul Williams, likewise. (*Looking round)* Hi everyone, nice to see you're hard at it.

Trevor

At this rate we'll be having a knees-up at The Savoy.

Steve

I did warn you.

Jeanette

(To Paul) Sonia will fill you in (everyone exchanges smirks). Oh stop this nonsense now; we have to get a grip and concentrate.

Soco 2

Ma'am I've found some remnants of a prawn near the frame.

Steve

You think our Tod was snacking on the job?

Paul

Sorry to interrupt, but have you found prawns anywhere else?

Soco 2

Only a bag in the fridge.

Jeanette

What's the significance, Paul?

Paul

Well, if they're kept near to his place of work, which in this case is the whipping room, they must be part of his modus operandi.

Steve

Never heard of anyone beaten with a bag of prawns, but whatever turns you on.

Jeanette

If anyone dares to say that something fishy is going on, I will sack them on the spot, understand?

Paul

If a punter's being humiliated, part of that process can be to feed them something they hate. Either making them vomit, or often if they do throw up, they are made to lick it up. This is to break their free will, and spirit. It's called 'desensitizing' or conditioning.

Jeanette

Nice work if you can get it.

Sonia

Trevor – could he have been forced into the bag?

Trevor

Seems unlikely without brute force being used. Like Steve says he was a boxer of some repute so he would have put up a tremendous fight. I'd tend to think it would have taken more than one person to effectively subdue him.

Steve

Very early on in his career Tod made the mistake of allowing a crazy punter to put a pair of handcuffs on him. He then attacked Tod with a Stanley knife, slicing a piece of his chest deliberately to scar Tod for life. Said he wanted to leave the mark of a master on him. He was never apprehended as Tod refused to press charges.

Trevor

That makes for a positive ID as I found the scar.

Sonia

So he's not likely to make that sort of mistake twice. But what if a gun was pointing at him, or a knife maybe?

Trevor

That could work but I'm sure he had a brain – even if it was a punch-drunk one and would have recognised danger when he saw it. Even so, I think he would have tried to escape and there are no marks on the bag to indicate that.

Sonia

So he could have either been unconscious or dead and put in the bag by two people or more?

Trevor

Probably. But don't forget he's been cooking on high heat for a week so we've lost a lot of evidence which is most likely why the heating was left on.

Jeanette

Why do I keep hearing that old Englebert Humperdink number: 'Please release me; let me go . . .'

Trevor

That's another quid right there just for the off-key rendition. Bit before your time wasn't it?

Paul

An interest in bondage and sado-masochism is usually related to childhood trauma. The individual tends to feel guilty when receiving pleasure. But they have the opportunity by surrendering themselves, to create a scene in which they are fully in control without realising it. They are recreating the feelings they felt in the early part of their life, but can change the ending. When in control they feel accepted and nurtured. It allows them to feel absolved of any responsibility, guilt or worry. It's about a struggle with life and the more dangerous the game, the greater the original disturbance. It can be a triumph over an early humiliation and a repetitive compulsion. Such extreme sex games which expose you to death, by taking life to the edge, provide a kind of release.

Jeanette

That makes a lot of sense Paul, thanks. Okay, the door was double locked and the person or persons who did that also turned the heat to full, opened the windows to ventilate the rooms, and if it was night time, turned off all the lights on exiting the building.

Sonia

So you're saying these people are forensically minded, calm, collected, methodical, and most of all cold-blooded killers?

Jeanette

Yes and the people who fall into that category are either professional assassins or people with strong enough motives and feelings of hatred to have planned this murder for sometime. What else can you tell us, Paul?

Paul

Well I am really excited by this one.

Jeanette

I hate to ask . . .

Paul

I saw his film on Channel 4. Me and my Slaves. 2006 I think. Fascinating from a psychiatric point of view. Here was someone who had spent over two decades at the top of a secretive profession who then does the opposite by confessing all in a cathartic broadcast on national TV.

Jeanette

So who would he have pissed off by going public?

Paul

More people than the suspect list for who shot J.R. that's for sure. Now, certain newspapers alluded that Tod was either a freemason or under the direct protection of someone who was. There's a lot of senior police officers particularly in the Met, who are masons.

Steve

That's nothing but a rumour and was never verified. You know that, Paul.

Paul

There's no way an operator of Tod's pedigree could have successfully plied his trade both in London and internationally without attracting the attention of law enforcement.

Steve

I was saying earlier we had linked him to the Trestrail scandal, two murders, and the spanner case. But in each case we had no conclusive evidence for us to take to the CPS.

Jeanette

I have to admit Steve, he seems to have been amazingly lucky to say the least.

Steve

(Looking down at the body) Well if that's him, his luck just ran out.

Paul

I also managed to get hold of a copy of his now banned book. Apparently Amazon insist on having six free copies of all books published as a proviso to being a distributor for any books coming onto the market. I sent off for one but had to pay double the cover price, but it was worth it.

Jeanette

So, just like Steve you're well acquainted with the life and crimes of Tod?

Paul

Tod and the numerous and diverse clients drawn to his specialized services all had one significant thing in common.

Steve

A shared distaste for fish?

Paul

No. But central to your understanding is to learn about compulsion. Compulsions are repetitive clearly excessive behaviors or mental acts, that the person feels driven to perform to reduce the anxiety caused by obsessive thoughts, or to prevent some calamity from occurring. Just look around this room for instance, the owner had everything in its right place, regimented, repetitive behavioral patterns showing clear signs of OCD – obsessive compulsive disorder.

Steve

How about him being just plain evil, Paul?

Paul

Evil consists in intentionally behaving in ways that harm, abuse, dehumanize or destroy innocent or in this instance, guilty individuals. It's using ones authority and systematic power to encourage or permit others to do so on your behalf. In short, it's knowing better but doing worse. That was Tod's job. His remit was to perform tasks that required him to act evil. Even if he was sane, and of sound mind. But that was his choice which was to meet his client's requests. To successfully maintain a master/slave relationship takes abilities and skills beyond or apart from, normal relationship skills. Although the master is understood to have authority over the slave in some sense. This never extends to ones legal rights. Thus there must always be an implicit element of consent involved. The control of the dominant over a sub is seldom absolute and often operates within a set of defined limits. However some forgo this option in the pursuit of extreme forms of edge-play. The Dom or Top is the actor who applies to the sub or bottom techniques of control, involving psychological activity, flogging, bondage servitude, torture captivity, humiliation, punishment and role-play. A top who acts a specific role for the bottom is known as a service top. A bottom who has dominance and controls the activities is said to be topping from the bottom. A role most clients naturally assume owing to the commercial side of the relationship. There is a temptation to dismiss S&M practices and their participants as a bunch of dysfunctional thrill seeking fanatics who have found coping mechanisms beyond our understanding. But we can't allow our own pre- conceived ideas or personal tastes to cloud our judgment. Otherwise this investigation will travel the same route that other historic cases have. Where lack of knowledge combined with natural predisposition, lead to open verdicts misadventure or even suicide. When in fact there has been a clear case of murder.

Jeanette

So Tod was a actor who performed dark scenes with fellow artist for the purpose of gain?

Paul

A rather simplistic view, but you could say he was making the most of his own somewhat disturbed background to try further his way in life. But his attention to detail along with the fact that people trusted him with their lives indicates that he had morals and a sense of duty of care to his clientele.

Jeanette

So despite appearances to the contrary you're saying he's not a sociopath?

Paul

Correct.

Sonia

This opens up an entire Pandora's box of human behavior we could learn from. That is if we want to. If Tod was alive I'm sure he would urge us to separate the evidence the same way he compartmentalized his life.

Paul

Exactly. After all, police officers use the same coping techniques to shut off their emotions when dealing with traumatic events. So do many other professions – doctors, nurses, counselors to name just three. This here is all about escapism and the Tod's of the world who supply that in this guise. For some of us it's a bottle of wine in front of the TV or an endorphin rush from a workout at the gym. For others – it's S&M.

Sonia

Tod took up boxing at 12. Could that have been part of his coping armory? And what if all those years of sustaining knocks to the head impaired his reasoning later in life?

Paul

Boxing careers usually end before a man hits mid life. But Tod carried on way past that. He couldn't let go – like he couldn't retire from S&M. Two fundamental issues which could have been on his mind at the time of his death.

Sonia

(flicking through book) Makes sense. Look at this page in his memoirs. The myth by which he had lived was starting to crumble. He floundered like a man who had lost his religion, and his confidence ebbed with faith. The sunshine of prior years shone less and less frequently. The clouds gathered so swiftly that it seemed as if they had come from nowhere. That was not the case. They had been forming on the horizon all along.

Paul

He's almost telegraphing his state of mind to the reader.

Jeanette

Thanks. We wouldn't normally have access to this kind of insight, Paul.

Paul

Not often I get the opportunity to get a close look at someone who's led such a complicated life. They don't usually stroll into my office and hop on the couch. Pity he's dead. Just one more thing – *(beat)* Tod spelt with one 'd' as in this case means death in German.

Steve

Tod by name and now Tod by circumstance.

Jeanette

Okay team – listen up! Scars aside Trevor will confirm that it is Tod we have in the bag by tomorrow. Aside from that, I would ask that you all set aside any pre-conceived ideas or prejudices. We have to be systematic and show tolerance and sensitivity in our investigation into Tod's life and what may after all, be his murder.

Trevor

I'm done here. We're ready to remove him if that's okay with you, Jeanette.

Jeanette

I was going to say tag him and bag him. But maybe my dark sense of humour isn't appropriate right now.

Trevor

Maybe it's your coping mechanism kicking in. Hopefully by tomorrow I'll be able to provide you with something more useful.

Soco 1

We've also found some tapes and a large amount of cash ma'am.

Jeanette

Where did you find them?

Soco 1

Under the chair – throne. Whatever you want to call it.

Sonia

What kind of tapes?

Soco 1

Professional format as opposed to your ordinary camcorder variety. There's reference codes on the cases. Some are marked audio only, others AV alongside the title "Me and My Slaves". Also on the case it says they've been filmed covertly spy cameras footage – court marshal scene.

Sonia

Same title as the cathartic film Paul said Tod had made. So, did they give Tod his own copies as a souvenir? Get them over to the labs ASAP and ask them to transfer them onto disc so we can run them back in the office. How much money did you find?

Soco 1

£15,000 in £20 notes all in a plain white envelope with no writing on it. It's not self-seal so we may get a DNA sample if someone licked it.

Sonia

(*Looking at plate on chair*) Presented to Brother Jackson GM. What does GM stand for I wonder?

Steve

Grand Master.

Jeanette

Good thing I have men on my team. The Masonic world isn't exactly female friendly. All those weird rituals. Not that I would want to take part anyway.

Steve

You might be a chief super by now if you were in the brotherhood.

Jeanette

What a nice thought. But I would also need a good handicap in golf.

Sonia

This chair seems very old. There can't be that many around. And why is it here. Surely Tod didn't have it as part of his apparatus?

Steve

My late dad was in the Hampstead lodge when he was a copper. So I got to learn quiet a bit about them. This throne is probably around 100 years old and made of fine oak. They didn't scrimp on the furnishings. You get one chair per lodge allocated to the Grand Master. Each time a new Grand Master is elected, they adopt the throne as the designated sign of power, so this might still belong to a current mason. They don't allow these symbolic relics to come on to the open market. Tod's been linked to the Masonic world more than once during his career. The main reason we believe he's avoided any criminal convictions. His Italian Duke was one Roberto Ferretti – a member of the infamous P2 lodge in London. This was the place of refuge Roberto Calvi fled to from Rome when he was on the run from the Vatican back in '82.

Jeanette

Remind me of that one again.

Steve

Basically hundreds of millions of lira had gone missing from the Vatican coffers. Calvi was known as God's banker because of his position as head of the Vatican bank. Ferretti and Calvi had grew up together in Milan. But a week after being holed up in London, Calivi contacted the P2 lodge to ask for help in evading the authorities in Rome. He was discovered hanging under Blackfriars bridge, his pockets filled with stones. Rough bricks indicate humiliation of a failed mason. One of the ancient penalties for breaking the Masonic oath was stoning.

Sonia

So are you saying Tod's Duke Roberto Ferretti betrayed his old school friend?

Steve

We'll never know for sure. But you can't ignore the possibility.

Jeanette

I want all the banknotes examined for traces of amyl nitrate. Maybe they were counted out during or just after the whipping session that left the blood and part of a prawn on the frame.

Soco 2

There's blood on this implement but it's not a whip. It's some sort of leather weapon

Steve

That's a Sjambok. It's made from rhino skin and was used exclusively by the South African police for riot control. Tod was very proud of this nasty piece. Back in '82 Tod met a former copper from Jo'burg who used him to recruit young desperate rent boys off the Dilly. They were known as 'chickens' by flesh-hungry punters. Lads who were desperate enough or just plain foolish to allow themselves to be thrashed by this deviant while Tod filmed. We found a number of copies of the tapes in a flat that we raided during the murder investigation of a punter of Tod's named Erskiene. Erskiene was a respectable young city banker. Yes ma'am I said banker. Tod had met him at a London gay boxing and wrestling club based in the East End. Tod would beat willing punters up like Erskiene in a proper boxing ring. And after leaving them bloodied and bruised, Tod would then remove his silk shorts and let the highest bidders sniff his sweaty jock strap. Tod used Erskiene to cash punters cheques through his bank. In 1983 Erskiene's body was found in two bin bags in a stream in Essex. His body was covered in injuries consistent to those shown on riot victims in South African police files. Tod was brought in for questioning and admitted knowing both Erskiene and his suspected murderer, the former South African policeman. But he'd already fled the country. Even though we suspected Tod had made a snuff movie of Erskiene being literally thrashed to death, when we tried to extradite the copper it was blocked by the Home Office who claimed it was too politically sensitive. So we had to return the sjambok to Tod as it couldn't be held as a murder exhibit if we couldn't proceed with a murder investigation. We had to let Tod have his trophy back because of beaurocatic policy making by the very same young politicians who probably utilised Tod's services.

Jeanette

It would be kind of ironic if our own enquiry into Tod experienced the same fate as Erskiene's. Kind of pay back time.

Steve

Nothing surprises me anymore. After all the years I've been on this job I'm beyond being fazed.

Sonia

A bit like Tod was to his line of work maybe?

Steve

Maybe. We are small fish in a big pond.

Soco 1

We've found a CCTV camera right opposite this building. With any luck we can get the tapes retrieved.

Sonia

That could provide a crucial break. Get it sorted ASAP. It's not why I joined the force but you get accustomed to certain crimes being hushed up for all sorts of reasons by a multitude of rich and powerful people.

Jeanette

Well until that outside intervention occurs we proceed full steam ahead. I want all the team assembled at 1600 hrs at HQ in Hendon for a de-brief and strategy meeting. (*Looking down on the hold all*) I wonder if you know just how much grief your death is about to unleash on people you knew.

Sonia

We'll get to the bottom of this. (*Looks at smiling officers and hands Steve £1)* Bugger, this is going to cost me a small fortune

End of Scene One

Act One

Scene Two

Gwen *(offstage)*

(*Beep beep*) "Hello you're through to Gwen. I'm not available at the present moment, but please leave a message or a number after you hear the tone." (*Beep*)

Tod *(offstage)*

Gwen, sweetheart. I keep missing you! Hey, I found this quote from a man I worshipped as a fighter but not as a God like the one we share. "A man at 50 who thinks the same way he did at 20 has wasted the last 30 years of his life." Muhammad Ali. I thought you said all boxers are as thick as pig shit? See you soon pussy cat.

End of Scene Two

Act One

Scene Three

The murder squad have regrouped for a briefing at their Hendon HQ.

Jeanette

Can I have your full attention please? I've decided that this case warrants a close-knit team of dedicated officers who are both determined and focused but above all who will not be fazed by whatever information comes to light. The nature of this man's death will throw up major challenges to our own perceptions about what is morally right and what is fundamentally perverse or evil. We'll all need to adopt a more tolerant mindset. One that will allow us to drawn on the knowledge from our enquires to develop a databank that we can utilise in future investigations. I want this team to be innovative in creating a template for other constabularies to exploit. Maybe it will ultimately help us in understanding this closeted area of human nature. Perhaps we will find that S&M practices are more to do with nurture. Whatever happens, we cannot afford to get side-tracked into unproductive areas that eat up manpower and resources.

Muttering accompanies this.
Jeanette holds up her hand for silence.

Jeanette

The point I wish to make perfectly clear is there is to be a closed shop on this one. By that I mean no talking to the press either from our own press office or personal contacts. We have to keep this one out of the public eye. The discretion we exhibit now will be rewarded in court later, if a crime has indeed been committed. You can imagine some of the hyped-up distorted stories that will circulate, if anything gets out. Tod was on the police radar for years and the file on his many near misses with the law looks like Encyclopedia Britiannica when it comes to evading prosecution. We don't want to end up answering awkward questions on cases we had nothing to do with by some know-it-all barrister out to undermine all our hard work. Don't forget – Tod was the subject of a broadcasted film on his life. Then there's the book which although supposedly out-of-print could become a major source of pain – no Steve, I am not paying for that one – should certain newspapers get hold of a copy. But let's be sure about one thing. If a murder has taken place, I will not let the nature of the victim's life style deter me from bringing those people responsible to justice. I will not waver in my duty even if it means upsetting certain people in key areas of government, the church or Masonic circles who have utilised S&M practices in their private lives. Now, until the body is formally identified by Trevor and the next of kin informed, we work with the evidence we have. Let's start with the scene. Gary, what have you got?

Gary

The flat is owned by a Sir James Gilfroy. It was purchased in 2005 for £450,000. No mortgage on the property so it must have been a cash purchase. There's no tenancy agreement and all the utility bills, insurance etc are in Gilfroy's name.

Jeanette

Are we talking about Sir James Gilfroy the former cabinet minister?

Gary

The very one ma'am. Multi millionaire businessman and ex-government trade minister. Resigned in 2006 citing personal reasons. Owns a very large manor house in Norfolk as well as a nice town house in Kensington. Currently sits on a number of boards of well-established companies. Married with a son and daughter. Regarded by the press as extremely well-connected and powerful.

Jeanette

Just the type of person I warned you we might encounter. What appears to be the relationship between Sir James and Tod?

Gary

Without jumping to conclusions there appears to be no apparent connections between Tod's previous encounters with the vice squad or the murder of Erskiene the city banker. Or the case of the murdered actor Peter Arne and the relationship he held with Sir James Gilfroy. Tod acknowledged in his book that Arne had been a client of his. He was found in his London home a short walk from Harrods in 1983. Particularly grisly murder as the crime scene photos graphically show. He had been chased around his home and then beaten to death with a poker. Tod wasn't a suspect but we heard whispers that Tod had known of Peter Arne's most recently acquired piece of rough trade – an Italian by the name of Giuseppe Perusi who had been sleeping rough in Hyde Park and selling his body for a hot meal and a warm bed. Arne got bored of him turning up at his door unannounced and had asked Tod to sort him out in return for a cash fee. Apparently Tod had some difficulty locating Giuseppe as the word got out that someone was looking for him. He probably assumed rightly that Arne was behind it and went round to his place in a rage to murder him. However he only lived another five days before he became a victim himself as his body was fished out of the Thames five days later. The verdict was suicide but we think Tod finally tracked him down and tried to recreate Roberto Calvi's hanging off Blackfriars Bridge but after a struggle ended up throwing the unconscious man into river where he drowned.

Steve

I was on the response unit who helped seal off the area when his body was recovered. There was substantial bruising and cuts to his body that were consistent with a sustained beating but got attributed his body being thrown around by the tides.

Jeanette

Steve, I realize I might be asking a lot here but could you try tracing any of your father's former fellow masons? And try to find out if Tod or Sir James Gilfroy have been or still are members of the brotherhood?

Steve

I can't promise you anything but I'll do my best.

Jeanette

We have to nail one of them to that Masonic throne found in Tod's apartment. Or should I say Gilfroy's flat? Are you certain Tod had no convictions only you said earlier he had been involved in a gun siege?

Gary

I've got that information here, ma'am. Tod was 19 at the time and living in a high rise in the red light district of Coventry, cohabiting with a convicted female prostitute of 27. Back then he was working as a council park keeper. His job brought him into contact with a retired gentleman with whom over the course of a number of weeks he had built up a strong enough friendship for them to share a drink in a local pub. The old boy was to use a euphemism – a friend of Dorothy's – meaning he was gay.

Jeanette

I think we all know what it means, Gary.

Gary

Right. Apparently the old poof offered Tod a large amount of cash in exchange for a fumble of his genitals in the toilets. The next hours were a blur, so Tod tells it. The old boy got him paralytic on strong lager and he was slipped some kind of drug in to his last pint. He woke up dazed. Half-undressed in a gardeners hut backed onto the park. He then makes his way home angry and confused. Some weeks earlier he'd bought a two/two rifle from a guy in a working men's club. He now used this to do his own Lee Harvey Oswald minus any grassy knoll and screaming with anger smashes the flat up. Girl friend escapes and calls the police. This was before today's armed response units so they storm the flat truncheons waving and Alsatians snarling to find Tod taking pot shots off the balcony. He gets jumped by about 10 officers, two of which win bravery awards. Tod was so off his head that they took him straight to psychiatric. No charges were brought because it was proved he had been drugged by an unidentified substance which led to his psychotic outburst. But Tod always maintained the police had beaten him up.

Jeanette

Which would explain why he has a grudge against the police.

Gary

(nodding) Mind you, he had anger issues way before this. His father abandoned him at nine and he never got over the rejection. He was raped by two men in a public toilet when he was 12. One of the men may have been his former teacher so we are talking major breach of trust.

Jeanette

Jesus. What happened?

Gary

He refused to ID the perpetrators but he freely admitted it was this particular crime that shaped his persona. So, as an adult he turns the tables using men as revenge, exploitation, financial gain and a way of acting out his own dark inner thoughts. Now along with the help and encouragement of the prostitute girlfriend, Tod could hone in on the most vulnerable but more importantly the most receptive men, to harness his natural anger and resentment. You could say his career path has been geared towards upward-mobility via developing the dark thoughts that he clearly held within himself.

Jeanette

Move over, Paul. Gary's got Tod's number. Sonia?

Sonia

Here's what a former punter wrote of him: 'You are a man of extreme passion. A hungry man, not quite sure where his appetite lies. A deeply frustrated man striving to project his individuality against a backdrop of rigid conformity. You exist in a half world suspended between two superstructures. One self expression and the other self destruction. You are strong but there is a flaw in your strength. The flaw? Explosive emotional reaction out of all proportion to the occasion.'

Jeanette

In other words the type of person who could murder and commit suicide.

Sonia

Maybe that's why he was so good at being bad. But he underneath maybe he was just as vulnerable as we all are.

Steve

Y'know I once pulled him over driving a customized van in Chelsea. Did a stop and search on him really just to piss him off. The van had blacked out windows and on opening the back doors I was shocked to find it kitted out as a mobile torture chamber. Fortunately for him there was no one tied up in there at the time. A smiling Tod freely admitted to starting what he called the 4th emergency service in London. Said the van was his MFU.

Sonia

MFU?

Steve

Mobile flogging unit. Couldn't help but admire his entrepreneurial flair if nothing else.

Gary

Guv, I've got some more on the Channel 4 film. Broadcast just the once in 2006. The film production company's credited as Pasolini Productions. The MD and owner is down as a Richie Wenton. Seems like he sold his company to a much bigger player – NCI Media just after completing Tod's film. It's all on YouTube but I've only had time to watch the first 10 minutes or so.

Jeanette

And?

Gary

What I saw was Tod beating a transvestite in a dungeon. With a males voice – I presume Richie Wenton, doing commentary. I scribbled a bit down: '65 strokes in 60 seconds. I am both shocked and disturbed. Tod clearly enjoys his work. And even though he says he is going to give it up. I am not sure he can.' Then the film breaks off to a commercial break. Which interestingly advertises dog biscuits, rubber gloves, antiseptic cream and weekend breaks to Amsterdam.

Jeanette

Give Richie Wenton a pull immediately.

Steve

Ding dong!

Jeanette

(Giving Steve a stern look) Hopefully we'll get to see the contents of those covert tapes found at the scene before we interview him.

Gary

I'm on it right now!

Sonia

I found a briefcase full of Tod's personal documents in the flat. He had three different current accounts all showing large cash withdrawals over the last 12 months. In fact all three were so heavily in the red that there is legal correspondence indicating that he was about to file for bankruptcy. Which is strange when you look at the rest which refers to a jointly held Swiss bank account, in both Tod's real name John Sweeney and a Roberto Ferretti. The same Roberto Ferretti who was friends with murdered Vatican banker Roberto Calvi. There has to be a link to the mason's here, don't you agree? The bank is E. Gutzwiller & Co. The manager is a Mr. Otto Dellenbach. I've spoken to his secretary but they won't discuss details of the account holders – not surprises there, so I don't anticipate us getting anything from them.

Jeanette

Seeing as the entire Swiss economy revolves around cuckoo clocks and secret banking, you're right. So, why would Tod be desperate for money if he's got access to a Swiss bank account?

Steve

But if Tod were desperate for cash then he might have been open to blackmail himself. It's something we haven't considered. Maybe he was in the process of handing those covert tapes to someone along with the 15 grand. However, it goes wrong and they kill him before he retrieved them from under the Masonic throne which they just didn't think to look under.

Sonia

Then why didn't they trash the place trying to find them? Maybe they had set him up to hand them over but their sole intention was just to murder him all along.

Jeanette

And placing his body in the bag was symbolic of their anger and contempt of Tod. As we know now the masons have historic rituals of murdering associates and leaving symbols that have reference to their past. Both the money and the tapes could have been left to deflect attention away from Tod's Masonic links. We need a breakthrough fast. Sonia – Google the name Pasolini. We are looking for anything that ties Tod into Italy, the masons or rituals. (*She answers the phone*) Please send him up. Paul Williams is here hopefully to educate us on the art of sado masochism

Gary enters carrying a disc.

Gary

The lab boys have come through. Here's the disc of the tapes found at the crime scene. Also we got lucky with the CCTV outside the apartment block. We've got a male and a female, both in their 20's outside the building at 3.45am. The male is carrying a bag.

Jeanette

Good one. Get e-fits made up and send out to all units via an internal bulletin.

Gary

I'll also circulate them to the other residents in the building.

Jeanette

Ok Steve, scan your porn pupils over this. You're our expert on section 63 of the violent porn laws.

Gary puts disc in laptop and presses the play button, a male voice is heard shouting.

Tod *(offstage)*

"Attention! Stand up straight you horrible little scumbag. I will read out the charges to this court marshal before announcing the punishment and hearing your plea of guilty or not guilty. Do you understand me you worthless dog?"

Sir James *(offstage)*

"Yes sir, understood sir'"

Steve

Fast forward Gary, till I say stop. We can't see the other mans face yet and I'm sure we can leave out the *Dad's Army* scene. Stop! Pause it right there where the old soldier turns round and gives us his best Benny Hill salute. Sonia – Google Sir James Gilfroy. Anything on his government career along with any press photos. From this angle it looks as if the camera is positioned in the ceiling.

Sonia

I've got a great one of Sir James addressing the party conference in 2003. I'll print it off.

Steve

If this is Sir James this would be paydirt for a blackmailer.

Sonia

There you go. Is it Sir James?

All bend down for a closer look.

Jeanette

So, is that a positive ID on Sir James? All those in favor raise your right hand. (*All of them raise their right hands, smiling*) I am trying my level best not to feel smug but I think I can safely say we have Sir James Gilfroy by the balls right now.

Steve

Play it again, Gaz. Let's see what the pillars of the establishment get up to in their spare time.

Gary hits play and Tod's voice is heard again followed by Sir James.

Tod *(offstage)*

"Remove your trousers before I cuff you to the frame you dog."

Sir James *(offstage)*

"Please sir, don't forget my poppers, sir."

Jeanette

Watch closely how he gives Sir James the poppers

Steve

And how close Tod has to get to him to administer them. There might be a cross- contamination at that point.

SFX: Heavy thrashing by Tod and screaming by Sir James)

Jeanette

Ouch! That must be doing some damage

Sir James *(offstage)*

"Boxer, sir! Boxer!"

Jeanette

I can't quiet believe what I'm seeing is consensual.

Steve

But boxing is just as destructive – if not more so. I don't want to sound as if I'm defending the likes of Tod, but Sir James is paying him to thrash the living daylights out of him. And did you notice? Tod stopped the moment Sir James said the safety or break word. In this case, 'boxer'. However, I can see blood dripping on to the floor.

His mobile beeps. He takes it out and looks at the screen.

Jeanette

Which makes it an offence of actual bodily harm. So if we go by the law as it stands, Sir James Gilfroy can be charged as consenting as we now know is not a defense. Bring in Sir James. Let's put some pressure on him.

Steve

Jeanette, I've just got a text from a contact of mine. Sir James Gilfroy has been a mason for at least 30 years. Not only that, but he is now a grand master.

Jeanette

Well, we are dealing with the big boys. So, the Masonic throne could belong to Sir James. But if so, why is it not at his lodge?

Steve

This might seem a little far fetched but Tod, Sir James and Richie Wenton were all connected by the covert filming. It's possible that they had a fixation on Pasolini's film *Salo* and were trying to make their own private version of it. Tod had been in a 15 year relationship with a very powerful Italian mason Duke Roberto Ferretti. This connection would have carried a lot of weight with Sir James. It gave him access to a deeper and darker Masonic world – yet another boundary to cross. Maybe all three of them wanted to honor their idol Pasolini with their own film.

Jeanette

The joint account Tod had in Switzerland. Could have been his payment pot? That went via the Duke straight from the Vatican itself. We could be looking at an international money laundering syndicate set up specifically for masons from all over the world to use to fund their vice addictions that also involved Masonic rituals.

Gary

Tod mentions in his book that at the beginning of 2005 he went to Basel in Switzerland and met an Otto Dellenbach who was head of the bank where his joint account was held. He was told all the monies had been withdrawn but that he had to leave the account open.

Sonia

That's who I spoke to over the phone who said he couldn't divulge any details. So, if Tod's pot of gold was stashed there this could only mean someone powerful had taken it. Ergo – Roberto Ferretti. If he could help Calvi rip off the Vatican then Tod would be small fry by comparison.

Gary

That's a fair assumption

Sonia

(*to Jeanette*) Boss, wait till you hear what I've discovered about Pasolini. "Pierre Paolo Pasolini born 1922 in Bologna. Poet, intellectual, philosopher, novelist, playright and extremely controversial filmmaker. Pasolini always showed his friends a virile strong exterior, totally masking his inner turmoil. In 1944 he was charged with the corruption of minors and obscene acts in public places which led to years of unemployment and being ostracized. His first novel "Ragazzi di Vita" (Rent Boys) was published in 1955. He also made a number of films which aroused controversy and scandal. In particular his last entitled *"Salo"* or *"The 120 Days of Sodom"* based on the writings of the Marquis de Sade. Pasolini was murdered in 1975 by being run over several times with his own car. Giuseppe Pelosi, a 17 year old rent boy confessed to the grisly killing only to retract his original statement in 2005. Turns out he was beaten and his family threatened to obtain it. Evidence uncovered since pointed to Pasolini being killed by a gang of extortionists. Testimony given by Pasolni's close friend Sergio Citti indicated that some footage taken during the making of his last film *Salo*, had been stolen. Pasolini had traveled recently to Stockholm to negotiate a buy back deal with the thieves who were threatening to blackmail him due to the compromising content of the stolen footage. They murdered him after he handed over a large cash deposit back in Italy. The stolen rolls of film were never found.

Jeanette

Richie Wenton named his production company after Pasolini for a reason. Maybe he's also a fan or maybe it has a deeper significance? See if we can get a copy of *Salo*. Perhaps Richie wanted Tod to help him replicate scenes shown in that film? And in return Richie paid Tod £15,000 as well as giving him the covert tapes Richie held of Sir James.

Gary

I'm on it.

Paul enters and sits down.

Sonia

Coffee, Paul?

Paul

Thanks but I'm totally caffeine'd out. Anymore and I'll be doing back flips in the corridor.

Sonia

I take it you've been up all night engrossed in the life and crimes of Tod?

Paul

Tod's John Sweeney's coping mechanism that he's used to navigate his way around the vice world. Tod allows Sweeney to separate himself from what he does. He's also a symbol of his own self-loathing. It probably all stems from him being raped in a public toilet by two men when he was 12. It led to a slew of deeply disturbing behavior patterns that were never addressed. So, Tod is born and it is Tod that allows him to express what he's feeling by pushing his own moral boundaries of what's acceptable. This allows him to go above and beyond the requirements of his clients who have varied tastes to say the least. As a torture-for-hire merchant he developed specialized skills and would go to extreme lengths to research his methods. Now these historic characters he researched became almost role models for him. Heroes to be idolized. But Tod was always striving to go one better. The more he performed these bizarre and deadly practices the more his own addictive personality kicked in. So he was as much a victim of his compulsions as his clients. However – the big difference for him was that he considered his work to be helping fellow compulsives achieve their own release if you like.

Sonia

So, you're saying that Tod is in fact a deviant form of sex therapist?

Paul

That's one way of looking at it. He's certainly performing a service.

All *groan.*

Steve

That's a quid right there just for a bad analogy.

Paul

I found some hand-written letters and answer machine tapes in with his personal documents all between Tod and a woman called Gwen Mulvey. Back in 2004, Tod was well on the road to self-destruction. He was drinking so heavily he'd begun to attend AA meetings at St. Thomas's hospital and it was at one of these meetings that he met Gwen. She was 64 and had been a chronic alcoholic for most of her adult life but in her early 20's had worked as a high class call girl. A friend of Christine Keeler, the notorious tart who was the catalyst for the Profumo scandal in 1963. After a decade as a hooker, Gwen found herself pregnant and addicted to class A drugs which she washed down with vast amounts of champagne. To survive she ran away with her young child to live in a Christian retreat named

Scargill situated in the Lake District. They supported her and her baby son for the next three years. She retrains as a psychosexual therapist and then moves back to London to set up her own very successful practice. But when her son grows up and leaves for university for some reason they lose touch and she slips off the wagon. She loses her home and her business and ends up living in a women's shelter. But looking at this, Gwen had become some kind of spiritual guide to Tod, even taking him to regular Sunday services at her local church. Here's one of the many cards she wrote to him: "My dear Tod, Forget the former things. Do not dwell on the past. Don't you realize how much you encourage me. And how I feel loved by you. God bless, Gwen." Now let me play you this tape – she must have meant a lot to him as he kept all the answer machine tapes.

Gwen *(offstage)*

"Tod darling I know you are struggling dear. Read Philippians 4/8. Firstly whatever is true. Whatever is noble. Whatever is right. Whatever is pure. Whatever is lovely. Whatever is admirable. If anything is excellent or praise worthy. Think about such things. When life gets a bit much. Remember what God says. You already think like this. Trust me when I say this. His holy spirit shows you so much. No one can ask more of you Tod. For I for one adore you. Hugs and much love, Gwen."

Sonia

It sounds to me that they were helping each other confront the fact that despite finding God, both had chosen immoral careers.

Paul

There's a sad end to this however. Gwen had been diagnosed with cirrhosis of the liver six months before she met Tod. As her health declined she started to rely on him more and more and a reversal of roles took place. She refers to him in one card as her 'gift from God'. Then it seems Gwen decided she didn't want to die a slow and miserable death. She begged Tod to take her to the Dignitas centre in Switzerland after she read about it in the papers. Dignitas would assist her suicide but Tod would not only have to foot the bill but also have to organize her immediate cremation, which was standard policy; and bring her ashes back to the UK. From their letters, Tod didn't want to do it. But when Gwen threatened to go alone, he relented. Tod now throws himself into the task of making Gwen's last days on earth as comfortable and meaningful as he can. A month before her death he even manages to locate her long lost son. I think this was a significant gesture on Tod's part. They were reconciled as mother and son even though it would be their last time together. Tod and Gwen flew to Switzerland in January 2005. He held her hand a she swallowed the poison that would end her life but before heading home he took a short detour to Basel.

Jeanette

And that's when Tod found out his secret stash of money had disappeared. But does it mean he was now so depressed after losing Gwen that he'd later consider taking his own life in some sort of symbolic ritual? And allow a film crew to record his downfall? In his *Me & My Slaves* film he had a pretty robust ego. But ego doesn't stand for Easing God Out. When was it filmed again?

Gary

April 2005 and broadcast a year later.

Paul

In the film he publicly revealed his relationship with Duke Ferretti. Okay he didn't name him but they showed a clip of them standing together in the main square in Brussels. But in the book Tod included all the details of the bank account which is why he self-published it. Not that any publishing house or literary agent would take it on. And having taken such a dangerous and provocative stance against the Masonic world, who comes along and buys the entire print run so nobody gets to read it?

Jeanette

Let me guess. None other than our old friend Sir James Gilfroy. After all, he's got the most to lose. Not only that – right now he's our number one suspect. Get me Gilfoy pronto.

Gary

On my way, guv.

Steve

I think I read somewhere that the Dignitas clinic is a small blue non-descript building situated on an industrial site well away from prying eyes. Isn't that what the Nazis did with their death camps? Hardly your usual Swiss chocolate box image. But then again, people snuff it every day in Luton. Seeing as it's the closest thing we've got to a concentration camp no wonder they want to check out.

Sonia

You really are one hard bastard Steve!

Steve

You 'd better believe it, doll!

End Scene Three

Act One

Scene Four

Lights dim. Gwen's answer machine is heard.

Gwen *(offstage)*

"Hello you're through to Gwen. I'm not available at the present moment but please leave a message or a number after you hear the tone."

SFX: Bleep.

Tod *(offstage)*

Gwen, darling. (*angry, slowly getting louder*) I'm sick of these bastards chewing me up then spitting me out.You know what it is. Betray is to be false, to break, violate, blab, tell, betoken, displaying, expose, discover, divulge, reveal, beguile, delude, ensnare, lure, mislead, corrupt, ruin, seduce, undo. I feel betrayed. *(The clatter of empty bottles then the sound of Tod falling off his chair*) Shit! I think I've over done the bubbly again.

SFX: Receiver is slammed down.

End of Scene Four

Act One

Scene Five

*Murder squad office. Enter **Trevor** and **Gary**.*

Jeanette

Good morning. Coffee's ready and waiting, boys.

Trevor

And good moaning to you too.

Steve

(*Placing a mug of coffee in front of Trevor*) Black, no sugar.

Trevor

Thanks, small addiction but very necessary.

Steve

According to our friend Paul we all have our compulsions. However, unlike the Tod's of this world I prefer to keep mine a secret.

Jeanette

Speaking of which – Trevor. Please put us all out of our misery and tell us what you know about our man in the hold all.

Trevor

Dental records confirm the body is that of John Sweeney – aka Tod.

Jeanette

Phew. I am actually relieved to hear that for the best of reasons. Sonia, do we know his next of kin?

Sonia

His mother. He also has two brothers both serving in the army. From what I can gather from his memoirs, Tod was cast from the family bosom a long time ago.

Jeanette

Okay. Send a family liaison officer around to the mother's address ASAP. Let them deliver the bad news. Looks like they won't be too concerned if he's really the black sheep he's made himself out to be in his book.

Sonia

Right away, guv.

Trevor

One more thing. Soco discovered a secret compartment in the Masonic chair some kind of commode or basin underneath the seat.

Jeanette

Don't tell me he had defecated on his throne and then closed the lid?

Trevor

No, but we did find what appears to be human ashes along with a suicide note.

Jeanette

So, you're saying Tod committed suicide?

Trevor

The note was written on a word processor and unsigned. We did get one of Tod's prints off it along with another set but they were smudged over by Tod's. Here –

Jeanette

Well I think it would be safe to assume the ashes are Gwen's that he brought back from Switzerland.

Trevor

I think that's the most likely explanation.

Jeanette

(*Reading note*) "There are few words that describe my sadness in leaving you this way. I want you to hold me close. To feel your strength as mine slips away. I want to make my last gaze to be looking into to your eyes that hold so much pain and heartache. Thank you for everything. We had a blast didn't we? I can't wait to show you that life begins when you decide to party with me in the after life. Goodnight, God bless. *Kiss, kiss, kiss.*" So is this Tod's suicide note or Gwen's goodbye letter to him? Or maybe the words of some warped client who Tod snuffed some time ago and he made them write this in case he was ever questioned? Along with the ashes this letter looks like a trophy and serial killers collect trophies. Steve – we need to look at two of Tod's former clients – Peter Arne and Richard Erskiene, both were found dead in strange circumstances.

Steve

Jawohl, mein kapitan. *(Gives a Nazi salute whilst clicking both heels)*

Jeanette

I'm beginning to think Steve is getting a little too close to the subject matter in this case.

Trevor

Well, he does carry his own handcuffs.

Jeanette

Don't we all?

Trevor

Speak for yourself. Anyway, back to business as they say. Tod was 50 years of age at the time of death. No external injuries or abrasions that indicated trauma of any kind. The only bruising found was on the elbows. The type of contusion in small clusters on these bruises indicates he was held by someone with small hands or was picked up by the same person just prior to or at the time of death. No sign of any struggle or of him trying to escape from the bag. A small amount of urine had been released into the bag but this can happen when the muscles surrounding the bladder relax and the body is moved at the moment of death. The Houdini squad or our friends at the National Policing Improvement Agency tell us the bag was made of a synthetic rubber called Neoprene. They calculated that within three minutes the temperature within the bag had reached 30 degrees Celsius and after half an hour the oxygen would have run out completely but that anyone getting into the bag would have been unconscious in as little as three minutes – roughly the same length of time as a boxing round. He had residues of vomit and saliva around the facial orifice and some was found in his hair. This had caused choking but not enough to bring about death itself. The vomit was contained around his head consistent with a bag being placed over it – not the hold all as no traces were found there or anywhere else in the flat. He'd come into contact with amyl nitrate and I can't tell if he had injested any prior to death.

Steve

Popper snorting, puking, S&M junkie!

Trevor

Nice try, Steve but nothing's conclusive here. Large amounts were found within his hair but he could have been administering it to someone else. No sign of any other drugs and there was a small amount of alcohol in his bloodstream equivalent to one unit. No signs of strangulation. Vagal inhibition had not occurred around his carotid artery. Pupils were not dilated.

Jeanette

So what killed him exactly?

Trevor

To be honest I can't tell you. I'd have to make an educated guess.

Jeanette

Okay – guess for me clever clogs (*smiling*)

Trevor

My theory is that Tod was with at least two possibly more, people. One being a female who was having her menstrual cycle. Part of the blood on the whipping frame showed she had been naked or partly undressed. The other blood sample wasn't Tod's or the woman's but probably the whipping victim's. Tod drank a glass of alcohol but no empty or partly drunk bottles of any kind were found either in the flat or in Tod's wheelie bin.

Steve

So a bottle may have been removed from the scene, thus indicating pre-meditation

Trevor

Sexual activity of some description took place between Tod and the woman. Her DNA was on his genitals.

Steve

So Tod got lucky. Ding Dong! Funny, I always had him down as queer but in hindsight I think Tod would have poked a coal fire if it didn't burn his tadger.

Trevor

Now here's the mystery, given Tod's reputation for being a professional control freak. For some unknown reason, he allowed himself to be restrained by the woman, she holding him by the elbows. The bruises were made by someone with small hands. Maybe in some sort of sexual practice or role-play scenario. He then becomes dizzy and disorientated long enough for a plastic bag to be slipped over his head. Maybe he was distracted by something else taking place between the other people in the room. He loses consciousness rapidly due to a combination of sexual activity, the heavy amount of poppers let off in a small, warm environment, the small amount of alcohol not to mention the ambient temperature. Added to that Tod was probably focused on keeping those around him pacified in some capacity. So, whoever did this to Tod clearly had intimate knowledge of the man's psyche.

Sonia

I have a gay friend.

Steve

Did you say gay friend or girl friend?

Sonia

What does that matter?

Steve

I just had you down as straight not some closeted diesel dyke.

Jeanette

Steve! This is highly inappropriate.

Steve

Well 'scuse me. I suppose 30 years working in vice has rubbed off on me. It's not like I'm shocked but if she wants to be a blokey type of copper then she can buy me a pint after work, we'll play a few darts, go to the bookies, drop some cash whist studying the form reading the Sun. Maybe follow it up at a lap dancing club where for 50 quid you get some cocaine snorting single parent from a broken home who ran away to the bright lights and ended up with some kebab shop owner who likes to give it her up the duck shoot. I'm going for a fag if that's alright with my new friend Ivor here. Well Ivor big one if you're interested. Oops, sorry. You like to down pints of real ale and talking shit whist you girl friend sucks on your pierced nipple. (*Storms out of office*)

Sonia

Wow – what brought that on?

Jeanette

I don't know. I've worked with Steve for 10 years and I have nothing but respect for his vast knowledge and experience. I've never seen him react like that and we have been in some truly awful situations. In fact, I can say hand on heart I wouldn't where I was today without his support and dedicated enthusiasm. It's totally out of character. I wonder if something is playing on his mind? I must apologize on his behalf, Sonia.

Sonia

No need. I can look after myself. I was pretty much a tomboy at school so I'm not adverse to grabbing a guy by his gooley gongs. But don't tell Steve I'm not gay. If he wants to judge a book by its cover then let him. Anyway, even if I was a friend of Dorothy we are living in the 21st century after all – I wouldn't have to hide it. Or be ashamed for that matter. Anyway – my gay friend. We went for a few drinks in Soho. Filled me in on poppers and other drugs that are regularly used in S&M scenes. He said Special K is a favorite.

Trevor

Ketamine? It's sometimes used by farmers to subdue bulls. It has the strength to knock them out. It's a short acting general anesthetic that has hallucinogenic and painkilling effects that can paralyze you.

Sonia

Yes, he said you are totally incapacitated by it. He also said that he's been in situations where vast amounts of poppers are used. This can lead to people who don't use becoming disorientated and confused before passing out completely. I then got him to buy a copy of Pasolini's *Salo* from a gay porn shop. Having watched the contents and reading the booklet accompanying it I can see why someone like Tod would be drawn to such imagery. The film is about a group of young men and women being imprisoned together in a large mansion out in the country. A group of four males are the masters who carry out systematic abuse and torture along with humiliation and sexual perversions on a vast scale. They encourage each other to go further and deeper in their exploitation of the prisoners. They use subtle brain washing to get them to eventually turn on each other leading to an orgy of brutal murders performed to the smiling masters who watch this chaotic scene unfold before their eager eyes. I think Tod would have used this film as a type of propaganda tool to encourage his clients to go beyond their normal limits. By brain washing them into thinking and acting like Pasolini he then would be in a much stronger position to exploit the now willing Pasolini devotees both physically and more importantly, financially. Now *Salo* was based on the writings of the Marquis de Sade. The notorious French nobleman who at school was brutalized with regular amounts of flagellation. This became his preferred method of torture on other people later in life. A failed search for a woman he had briefly fallen in love with sent his mind into exploring devious forms of sexual perversion. He was sent to prison for these acts at the age of 23. Of his remaining 51 years he spent 27 of them in prison where he did most of his writing. Eventually he was sent to an asylum. He was described as being handsome, charming, polite, well-groomed and sympathetic towards women. All these attributes could be Tod in a different era.

Gary

Sorry to interrupt ma'am – but we've brought in Richie Wenton, he's downstairs in reception. Steve is with him now, shall I send them up?

Jeanette

Yes, let's talk to Wenton before he gets a lawyer. I'll need to have a word with Steve later though. Trevor, do you mind?

Trevor

Not at all. I think we've covered off everything for now. If I come up with anything else I'll let you know. I'll want to open the inquest as quickly as possible as I've got a massive backlog of cases and well – there's only one of me. *C'est la vie.*

Jeanette

Et mort. We've had 50% of our budget cut so now we can only prioritise the cases we think will yield a positive result. And I'm afraid this one isn't falling into that category. Be in touch Trevor and thanks again. (*Trevor leaves just before Steve and Richie Wenton enter*) Mr. Wenton please take a seat. I'm Detective Chief Inspector Jeanette Somber. This is DS Sonia Whitehead. Over there is DC Gary Griffiths. And last but not least DS Steve Miller.

Richie

(*Looks angrily at Miller*) Yeah – we've got a history.

Jeanette

Really? Enlighten me?

Richie

Well, we go way back don't we, Steve? He and I are old school. *(winking)*

Steve

Shut the fuck up, Richie. Your mouth needs filling.

Richie

Oooohh! Who's getting cranky in his old age?

Jeanette

Mr. Wenton —

Richie

Call me Richie, darlin'. We don't have to be formal do we especially as I'm amongst friends, eh Stevie boy?

Steve

I won't warn you again, Wenton.

Richie

To you it's Mr. Wenton, you bastard.

Steve

And to you it's Mr. Bastard.

Jeanette

Okay, that's enough. You're here to help us with our enquires into the death of John Sweeney aka Tod.

Richie

Yeah, I heard he had bit the dust don't expect any tears from me though.

Jeanette

You heard about it where exactly?

Richie

I was taught to be discreet (*pauses whilst looking at Steve*) but as I'm here I might as well tell you a journalist phoned me yesterday and told me Tod has now departed to hell to visit his old deviant friends. Guess he wanted a comment as I'd documented his notorious life on film. I told him no comment (*looking at Steve*) – for now.

Jeanette

Which paper was he from Richie? And do any others know yet?

Richie

That would be telling officer and I don't tell tales

Sonia

Neither do dead men, Richie. Now at the moment you are not a suspect.

Richie

Suspect in what officer? You saying Tod was done in or something?

Sonia

I thought you said you heard about Tod's death from a reporter?

Richie

I did but he didn't say how he died. He just wanted to know how the film had affected Tod and if it played a part in his death.

Jeanette

I'd advise you to answer our questions honestly, Richie. You wouldn't want to perjure your self in court at a later date.

Richie

Court! My hairy arse! Please tell me you lot are kidding?

Steve

This could be a murder case, Richie. How would you like to end up naked and dead in a bag?

Richie

Is that how he died? Thanks for that. I might be able to do a little trade with the papers. I owe you a pint, Stevie boy.

Gary

Richie, can you tell us when you last saw Tod alive?

Richie

I think it was about two weeks ago.

Gary

So a week before he died?

Richie

Nice try, son! But I don't know when he died or how for that matter.

Sonia

For someone who worked closely with Tod for at least 12 months filming his personal and business life you don't seem the least bit upset that he's dead.

Richie

That thieving runt tried to ruin me by getting Channel 4 to go to court. Alleging that I conspired to film a certain member of parliament in very compromising circumstances with the intention of blackmailing the victim at a later date.

Steve

Well you did, and we have the covert tapes to prove it.

Richie

You have the tapes now? I got NCI media to release those tapes to the victims lawyer on the understanding they would be destroyed and that would be the end of the whole sorry saga. But greedy, needy Tod duped the lawyers with counterfeits whilst using his best charm to butter up the lawyers long enough to distract their attention whilst he made the switch right under their snotty noses. Tod spent 15 years with an Italian duke who groomed him to be the personification of the devil himself. Part of which was to always have something on a client that you can use at a later date to blackmail them with. Tod made more dodgy films than I made programmes in my whole 30 year career.

Sonia

Richie, are you aware that filming covertly without their knowledge is a jailable offence? Last month a BBC producer got six months for filming himself having sex with various girl friends, who were totally unaware of a camera placed in a ceiling fan. Under section 79 of the sexual offences act it's called voyeurism.

Steve

You're certainly guilty of voyeurism. And if we can prove you also blackmailed a certain Sir James Gilfroy when you made the covert tapes of a court marshal scene – the contents of which contravene section 63 of the current violent porn laws. That's three strikes right there. On top of all that – should we find that your DNA matches samples that were found in Tod's apartment at the time of death you'll also be charged with murder.

Richie

Have you ever considered colonic irrigation?

Steve

Why fuck face?

Richie

Because you are so full of it.

Steve launches himself at Wenton, pinning him to the desk. He raises his fist but doesn't strike. Steve shouts he will kill Wenton as the others pull him away. Wenton laughs.

Jeanette

Steve – I want you to calm down or leave, okay?

Steve

You're the boss.

Richie

How does it feel Stevie boy with big girly ordering a macho man like you about? Bit of a come down eh, luvver boy? You should be careful Mr Bastard, only this case might open all our secret closets. Now that would make the headlines.

Jeanette

Less of the big girl if you don't mind.

Sonia

Why did you make the film on Tod's life anyway? Did you know him before then?

Richie

I met Tod in 1980 when I was a journalist for boxing weekly. Not long after I became a sub-editor at the News of the World.

Gary

So was it you who did the Commander Michael Trestail exposé?

Richie

You bet your sweet ass it was. Tod was a fairly new piece of meat working the 'dilly when he was asked to do Tressie as a one off-treat from his regular "renta" called Rauche. But Tod had a sharp instinct for a story as well as a deep hatred for the police. He made a quick 10k and I made a big impression with my new employers. Isn't that right, Steve? After all you were then a young handsome PC who had picked Tod up a number of times for importuning. Wonder why you could never get the charges to stick Steve? (*Steve ignores this*)

Gary

Did you pay Tod to do the film for Channel 4?

Richie

To be honest I did promise him £15,000 on completion of the agreed two broadcastings by Channel 4. But they received so many complaints about its contents they decided to cancel the second showing and deducted 30 K from my commissioning fee of £150,000. Which effectively wiped out my profit margin overnight. Neither Tod nor I made a penny from it.

Sonia

How did Tod react to not being paid for a film that made him vulnerable to police prosecution? Not to mention him pissing off his Masonic connections as well as those in the Vatican. These are people who have the ability and resources to resort to professional assassins.

Richie

Tod was already drinking way too much by the time we started filming. He was already depressed over the death of Gwen Mulvey. I would have liked to have included her in the film but she was already dead and life's a bitch eh, Steve? Pity though. An old tart like her croaking it at a clinic in Switzerland. Would have made great TV! He kept ringing me up threatening me with all sorts of painful punishments but I don't frighten that easy. Besides I knew that behind the master's mask was just a disturbed and abused boy. He was very subdued and as much as I admired his flawed logic of honesty and openness being his way to redemption, it was a mistake. Transparency doesn't equal forgiveness. I just wasn't prepared to be his kind of whipping boy when something happened that was beyond my control.

Sonia

Getting the tapes released to Sir James Gilfroy's lawyer meant you'd fulfilled your legal obligations. But Tod having stolen those tapes before Gilfroy received them now meant he could get you jailed if he wanted to, yes?

Richie

Yes, but he didn't do that did he, officer?

Sonia

No he didn't and that's my point. He could have blackmailed you for the £15,000 you owed him.

Richie

But again, he didn't.

Sonia

So the £15,000 cash we found at Tod's address wasn't from you?

Richie

I haven't got a pot to piss in. Don't you understand I'm about to go belly up financially?

Sonia

And morally.

Richie

Infamy infamy, everybody has it in for me! (*Laughing, stands up with arms held aloft*)

Jeanette

I think we'll postpone this interview for now. Gary, take him down. And book another interview in reception the day after tomorrow.

Richie

That's right m'lud, take him down (*laughing as he is led away*). I can always flash the judge one of those masons in distress signs should you get me in court. You know all about them don't you, Stevie boy?

Sonia

Richie, you're free to go!

Richie

Go where? Home? The pub? The supermarket? The porno house in Soho with the creaky seats that give your wrist movements away?! Maybe the bank I have no money in! How about the church that I don't confess my many sins in? Or go to the jobcentre where there are no jobs, just bored underpaid staff singing the same mantra: *sorry have you ever thought of higher education?* Except that costs 10 K a term now! Go anywhere, and my problems go with me officer. I can't escape what's in here (*pointing to his head*) and what's missing in here (*points to his heart*).

Gary finally pulls him out the room.

Jeanette

Steve, what's got in to you? Are you having your own midlife crisis or is there something you're not telling me about you and that slime ball Wenton?

Steve

Are you questioning my judgment or just my poor fighting skills?

Jeanette

You revealed details of Tod's death that Wenton didn't know. You actually named Sir James Gilfroy even though we had called him a victim up to that point. And then you threaten to charge Wenton with murder before we have even done a swab test on him for his DNA profile. Should this case ever get to court his lawyer will suggest we acted outside legal requirements thus making a conviction for any crime impossible. Why don't you take some time off?

Steve

Is that an order boss?

Jeanette

More of a suggestion. I want you on this case. You've years of tracking Tod's vice career and that's invaluable to me.

Steve

Fine. I'll see you in the morning.

Steve EXITS.

Sonia

Don't you think he's a liability right now? He's clearly got a history with Wenton as well as being out-of-control, arrogant and homophobic.

Jeanette

Are we talking about Steve or Tod?

Sonia

Say what you like about Tod but at least he's not homophobic. He just exploited men full stop. A straight man willing to sell his body and violent skills. Gay for pay is what it's known as.

Jeanette

What a buck for a suck or a lira for a queera?! That's a sound observation and observation is a faculty worth cultivating. Anyway I need Steve on this particular case. He holds more than one key to solving this puzzle. Come on, we've work to do. Just another day in the dirty office. No rest for the wicked, eh?

Sonia

Only the ones that are dead.

End of Scene Five

Act One

Scene Six

SFX: Beep beep

Gwen *(offstage)*

– Hello you're through to Gwen. I'm not available at the present moment but please leave a message or a number after you hear the tone. (*Bleep*)

Tod *(offstage/drunk)*

Hiya sexpot! (*singing*) I beg your pardon. I never promised you a rose garden. Along with the sunshine. There has got to be a little rain sometime. When you take you got to give so live and let live. Or let go –whoa-whoa –whoa. (*Laughing, abrupt hang-up*)

End of Scene Six

Act One

Scene Seven

In a cheap Travelodge Richie Wenton pulls a bottle of Scotch from an overnight bag on the floor. Retrieving the tooth mug he pours a large measure and downs it in one before pouring another. He starts to undress and removes lingerie from the bag – a basque, bra and frilly knickers which he puts on. After applying make up and donning a wig he dials a number on his mobile.

Richie

Hi it's Claudia. I'm ready, willing and very able. Sorry? (*listens*) Then go outside and ring me back in five minutes!

He pours another drink while he adjusts his make-up. His mobile rings.

Well how was I to know your domestic arrangements had changed? (*beat*) I was really up for it as well. Come round now and you can have me for your pleasure. (*pauses, smiling*) Can't you just sneak out for a quickie? (*beat*). So what am I going to do now ring for room service? (*beat*) Oh very funny big boy! Dead men can't speak or fuck but that will hardly bother a stud like you. Just tell her you have to see a guy about a dog or something. I am at the Travelodge we used last time (*pause, fiddles with wig*). You can tie me up again. You know how horny you get doing the rape scene. (*beat*) You promise? You know you shouldn't keep a girl waiting. (*beat*) Okay hun, see you soon, I'll leave the door on the latch and pretend I'm sleeping like last time, remember? (*beat, smiles stroking crotch*) Of course you do, 'bye hun.

He takes another shot and dials another number.

Hey, it's Richie can you talk? Look I was interviewed today at Hendon. Well you should bloody know that's where the murder squad is based. They asked about the tapes. They found them under that bloody throne of his. Yes, and the money you stupid bastard. Why didn't you look harder? I was too busy getting Bonnie and Clyde out of the flat. And if you haven't destroyed the film we did then, you might as well go fucking top yourself, unless you want to serve the rest of your days in jail! (*beat*). Then we'll both go down for this! (*beat*) Oh yeah, you reckon do you? Well listen carefully, master misfit. It won't take them long to work out the Pasolini connection. My company was named after him under your instructions or have you forgot that as well as the rather small detail that you were a major shareholder? Your brothers at the lodge can't get you off this time. Remember Calvi ended up swinging under Blackfriars Bridge? Are you a good swimmer with bricks in your pockets? They will abandon you just as they did with that evil scum bag Tod. Why don't you reflect on his death? Neither of us want that indignity do we? If you force me into a corner this is one canary that will start singing, you catch my drift big man? (beat) I will testify in court that wasn't the case. You know I am the only one who can get you out of this mess. There is going to be a scandal anyway so look upon me as a damage limitation exercise. (*beat*) It's not a case of guilt by association if I am willing to say something to the contrary.

Laughs, sips drink.

Okay, I'll settle for seventy five that's bloody half price! You got us on a two for one deal, you slag (*beat*). Of course I'm desperate and you know it. But feed a starving dog and it won't bite (*beat*). You can afford it so stop winging. Room 301- I'll leave it unlocked. Just because it's our last time doesn't mean Claudia doesn't get her lollipop. (*beat, strokes crotch*). I thought that might tempt you. You think God gave me lips like these just to suck on oranges? (*beat, smiling*). I will be a naughty girl for you, master. You know you can pull my hair and tell me what a dirty bitch I am (*laughs*) Oh sir, I will try to swallow everything sir. I'm sooo sooo thirsty... Look I'm at the Travelodge again so why don't you bring me what I want and everything will be sorted? It's just after nine now but I should be free by midnight. Okay hun, 'bye. See you for a sucker supper.

End of Scene Seven

Act One

Scene Eight

The beep of Gwen's answer phone.

Gwen *(offstage)*

Hello you're through to Gwen. I'm not available at the present moment, but please leave a message or a number after you hear the tone. (*Beep*)

Tod *(offstage/very drunk)*

I could promise you things like big diamond rings. But you don't find roses growing on stalks of clover. So you better think it over. Well if sweet talking you could make it come true. I would give you the world right now on a silver platter. But what would it matter. So smile for a while and let's be jolly. Love shouldn't be so melancholy. Come along and share the good times while we can. (*Tod breaks down crying in deep, drunken distress*) Oh, Gwen when will the pain ever go away? (*Receiver is slammed down*)

End of Scene Eight

Act One

Scene Nine

SFX: police sirens. Flashing blue lights strobe the background. The Travelodge room is now a crime scene. in the background police sirens can be heard. The Travelodge room is now a crime scene with Richie's body lying face-up on the bed with a plastic bag over his head. Attending are our two Soco's, Trevor, a PC and the Tod murder squad.

Jeanette

What do you think, Trevor? Accident or suicide?

Trevor

Well, he's had sex with one possibly two men in the last 24 hrs. Soco's found discarded condom wrappers in the bin. Both different brands but rather interestingly no used condoms.

Steve

Perhaps he ate them. Tod once told me when he was running a male sauna he sold all the discarded condoms to a young fellow who let's say had a strong taste for rubber chewing gum.

Sonia

Yuk! You sure you're not just making this stuff up to try to shock us, Steve?

Steve

If you knew Tod when he was alive then you wouldn't doubt anything I say.

Sonia

Sounds like you were fond of him – as well as being repulsed by him.

Steve

What you saying exactly? That I'm as queer as you?

Sonia

I just happen to have those feelings about Tod myself, that's all. I can't help think he was a demon who enjoyed doing unspeakable acts. But the other side of his personality is just so engaging. I feel drawn to him either way.

Trevor

Like the devil in disguise. Getting back to our man here or should I say shemale? There are large traces of disinfectant around and inside the mouth. I can't tell if it was poured in before or after death yet but the most likely reason for using it is to act as a masking agent, to hide bodily fluids in the mouth.

Sonia

In other words he was performing oral sex on someone?

Trevor

Yes. There's a bottle of Domestos over there. It does what it says on the label, kills all known germs dead.

Steve

I didn't know Wenton was German?

Trevor

Your jokes get worse, Steve. We can't rule out that it's not some symbolic sign.

Steve

What a Mason who swallows is a non-fussy eater maybe?

Trevor

Don't give up the day job, Steve. There's a can of ethyl on the side here. Its effects are similar to poppers but it can be a lot stronger for the novice user to handle. There was a strong smell of it when I lifted the bag on his head and a large amount of vomit in the bag. Looks like he choked on it when he inhaled it back down his windpipe. Very unpleasant way to go.

Jeanette

Why didn't he just remove the bag when he started to choke?

Trevor

His hands were cuffed behind his back.

Jeanette

That kind of rules out suicide.

Steve

So he was having sex with one or two males. Bit of rough trade maybe? If they weren't using condoms it's known as 'bare backing'. And in the heat of the moment he choked and suffocated having ingested the ethyl while the rough riders were too busy busting his bum to notice. Rodeo over and they find Calamity Jane here has gone and snuffed it so they leave him here for us to find. Inconsiderate bastards. Wonder if Richie was the trannie we saw in *Me & My Slaves* in Tod's dungeon? I'm just waffling, ignore me. But that's life and shit happens.

Trevor

I don't agree with your sentiments, but I have to admit it makes sense.

Jeanette

Do we have any CCTV of anyone seen entering? (beat) The room, Steve.

Steve

(Clearing throat, composing himself) Yes, guv. I've already sent the tapes back to Hendon for analysis. Only problem is they got chewed up taking them out of the machine and I'm not sure the lab boys will be able to play them.

Jeanette

Terrific. Then we don't have much to go on. The male studs won't want to come forward. They probably met through a dodgy website or even 'cottaging' at the local train station.

Sonia

No wonder Richie's head was all screwed up if part of his persona was as a cross-dressing slut who picked up strangers for no-questions-asked sex

Trevor

I think we're done here, Jeanette. I'll send you the toxicology report and the exact cause of death. I'm loath to admit it but this one has all the hallmarks of accidental death. A misadventure verdict seems the most likely outcome.

Jeanette

You know I always respect your opinion, Trev. Are you ok? Only you seem a bit weary today.

Trevor

Half my budget slashed, a backlog longer than a traffic jam on the M25. I have to tell four of my best soco's that their expertise and most of all, undivided loyalty is no longer required and my wife and best friend of the past 38 years has just found out she has breast cancer. Apart from that – oh, wait. My car has a flat battery due to me absent-mindedly leaving my headlights on all night. But really, I'm just dandy, Jeanette. But thank you for asking. No one else can be bothered to notice.

Jeanette

Trevor – please take care.

He shrugs and EXITS head down.

Jeanette (con't)

Phew. This is all getting too much.

Steve

If you can't handle the heat, get out of the oven, boss. Let's not expend too much time and effort on Wenton, the tart with no heart.

Sonia

Steve – please don't take this the wrong way.

Steve

What?

Sonia

Shut the fuck up

Steve

Ouch! Easy me old mate

Jeanette

Wenton was a major link into Tod's death. We have to go for the next in the firing line.

Sonia

That has got to be the beaten squaddie in the hurt locker – Sir James Gilfroy

Jeanette

Between you and me he represents our only hope for solving this case. Otherwise Tod and Wenton will just both be remembered for their sad bizarre deaths and nothing else. Time for a change in tactics. Let's see how he reacts if he's made to answer questions sitting in his gothic monstrosity of a house. Yes – he'll be in his comfort zone physically but you know what they say – never shit in your own nest.

Sonia

I can give you some famous names to go with Tod and Wenton. Michael Hutchins, musician. Roberto Calvi, Vatican bank director. David Carradine, actor. Sal Mineo, Actor. Krystan Digby TV presenter. Rod Hall, talent agent. Peter Arne, actor. Steven Milligan, MP. Alexander McQueen, fashion designer. Piere Palo Pasolini, Film maker

Jeanette

Don't forget the not so famous but as equally as important – Gareth Williams, MI6 spy. Richard Erskien, banker. Darren White, businessman. John Sweeney known simply as Tod, professional S&M dungeon master. May their souls all rest in peace.

Sonia

Amen to that.

SFX: Jeanette's mobile. She answers it.

Jeanette

Okay. Thank you for letting me know.

Sonia

You look like you've seen a ghost. Bad news?

Jeanette

That was the family liaison officer back from visiting Tod's mother.

Sonia

And?

Jeanette

The entire family are united in one opinion. That none of them will acknowledge Tod's existence in any way, shape or form. As far as they're concerned, Tod died the day he was raped by those two men in a toilet. They say they won't even attend his funeral should he be having one. Their hate is so strong that they even said we should have left him in the bag to rot.

Sonia

My God – how awful! It's as if he had become a total leper.

Jeanette

(losing it) It makes me uncomfortable just to hear it. Well, who needs enemies when you have family? God! Life can be really crap at times.

She puts her head in her hands, starts crying. Sonia puts her arms around her at the moment Steve enters. Seeing them in a quiet embrace he takes a photo using his mobile phone, turns and leaves quietly without them noticing.

Sonia

This isn't just about Tod, is it? What's upset you so much?

Jeanette

My husband announced late last night that he's moving out, to live with a young piece of skirt he met on a work 'bonding' weekend last year. Well they bonded alright, just about stuck together like super glue. I should have seen it coming really. My kids don't know me anymore; I think I'm heading for the menopause already. My last period was God knows when. Do you know I panic before I sneeze or laugh now, because I'm afraid I'll wee my pants? So I now wear those little soaking hammocks called panty liners. I had a coughing fit in the office the other day. I had to keep launching myself off my chair in a rhythm of cough pee cough pee until I stopped, bloody knickers were wet through. Any last shred of dignity I have has all been taken away from me. I've put on two stone in weight just comfort eating. And all the while my mind keeps running through three other murder cases that I have on the go as well as Tod's. It all seemed so good at one point. Career on the up, two healthy kids, husband working whose only vice seemed to be a season ticket to West Ham. We would have two foreign holidays a year and I paid my credit card off in full every month. We had sex in more than one position at least once a week. Happy days! Now everything has gone tits up, but I still have to maintain this cool calm exterior for the sake of the force.

Sonia

Right – grab your bag, turn your phone off because I'm taking you for a big drink and a blubbing session. And before you say no because you're paranoid about the chain of command being compromised think of how Todd and Gwen were there for each other. Besides, the world takes on a better shape over a bottle of Cab Sav. Oh, and one more thing. I went through a civil wedding with my partner of eight years last summer in Prague. She is going to love playing mother hen to you and it will give her a break from having to listen to my problems. Come on before you start panicking thinking you've let your guard down too much. The whole world can wait. Let's face it – we're all hypocrites whether we're straight or bent.

End of Scene Nine

Act One

Scene Ten

SFX: Beep!

Gwen *(offstage)*
Hello you're through to Gwen. I'm not available at the present moment, but leave a message or a number after you hear the tone.

Beep.

Tod *(offstage)*
(*Clearly in distress*) Gwen, my angel. Matthew 8- A man with leprosy came to him and begged on his knees "If you are willing, you can make me clean." Filled with compassion, Jesus reached out his hand and touched the man. "I am willing," he said. "Be clean." When will I be free of the dirt I roam in Gwen, you tell me?

Music Up: The last verse of 'Rose Garden' by Lynn Anderson

INTERVAL

Act Two

Scene One

Sir James Gilfroy's Norfolk mansion. The murder squad are shown into a large drawing room by Gregory, Sir James's butler.

Gregory

Sir James will be with you in a moment. Please do be seated. May I offer you refreshments? Perhaps some Earl Grey for the ladies?

Jeanette

Thank you, but I think we'll skip the pleasantries if you don't mind.

Gregory

Very well, madam. I shall remind Sir James that you are waiting for him.

Jeanette

Please do. Time is of the essence.

Gregory

Indeed it is, madam.

Gregory EXITS.

Steve

Well smack my arse and call me Charlie. So this is how ex government ministers live in retirement.

Gary

Go easy, Steve. I wouldn't say this was typical. Sir James has a portfolio of interests in various companies.

Steve

Wonder if he's doing a 'Richard'?

Sonia

What's that? Another one of your vice squad sex stories?

Steve

Not far off the mark my dykey friend. Richard Branson owned one of the biggest gay night clubs in London. For years he provided a venue called Heaven for men to meet up and have unprotected sex. Then when Aids first hit the scenes in the early 80's he then bought out the London Rubber Company, that's a condom company by the way, not racing tyres. Gave out free samples during swinging club nights. Fuck 'em in, fuck 'em out, then fuck 'em off. Talk about making it at both ends.

ENTER Sir James Gilfroy. All stand to greet him.

Jeanette

Sir James I'm Chief Inspector Jeanette Somber. This is Detective Sergeant Sonia Whithead. That is Detective Constable Gary Griffiths and next to him is D.......

Sir James

Detective Sergeant Steve Miller.

Jeanette

You two know each other?

Sir James

We attend the same lodge, as well as does your boss Detective Chief Superintendent George Frankish. Who I also like to beat on a regular basis! (*pauses for effect*) At golf, dear. What ever did you think I meant?

Jeanette

Why didn't you tell me Steve?

Steve

You didn't ask.

Sir James

Do sit down officers. I can give you no more than 30 minutes. My wife is due back then. And I wouldn't want to distress her by the sight of the Met visiting me mob-handed.

Sonia

Interesting turn of phrase. Mod handed. Any Italian connections there, Sir James?

Sir James

It's no secret that some of my subsidiary companies are based in Italy.

Sonia

Whereabouts in Italy, sir?

Sir James

Milan actually. Why?

Sonia

What type of companies may I ask?

Sir James

No you may not ask. That is, unless my lawyer is present. Which as you can see he isn't. Can I get you some refreshments sent up?

Sonia

I don't like Earl grey it gives me thrush.

Sir James

(*smiling*) Try drinking lemon barley, my wife swears by it. I'm a Pimms man myself.

Sonia

I can't imagine your wife saying 'this fucking lemon stuff is bob-on, darling'.

Sir James

You're both naughty and nice, I like that in a girl.

Gary

What about in a man, sir?

Sir James

I beg your pardon?

Gary

We have covert filming taken during the production of a film entitled *Me & My Slaves*, made about the life and crimes of a man known as Tod. Is that naughty enough for you, sir?

Sir James pours a Pimms and ice and sits down. He remains silent.

Gary

Why don't I read some of the texts we found off an "S-J" on Tod's mobile. "That heavy one strikes me as fit for purpose, enabling my sadistic master to break his willing dog. S-J" "Sir, do you want me to do bullying for next week? Dress in number two's and best boots, Sir S-J" "Sir, wife not coming to London on Monday, so hope your dog can still come as he urgently needs his masters discipline S-J." S-J wouldn't stand for Sir James by any chance?

Jeanette

Would you like to comment on that, sir? Or should be wait until your wife gets back to play them for you on our laptop? Or should I get those nasty images broadcast on *Crimewatch* to see if any viewers can identify the person bent over Tod's whipping frame? You really should get that sweat rash attended to, sir!

Sonia

Should yield something, guv, even if it's just a few laughs.

Gary

No, I think someone in Milan might just recognize their managing director as we have a full facial shot at the end. When Tod is rubbing his hob nailed boots over the willing victim's nipple clamped chest. That scene always sticks in my mind for all the wrong reasons. Not everybody's cup of tea – even the Earl grey variety

Sir James

(*Slamming his fist on the table*) That's enough! *(holds hands up)* Okay. What exactly do you want from me?

Jeanette

I want the truth. Is that you in the covert film with Tod?

Sir James

If I say yes will you look to prosecute for the illegal practices shown?

Jeanette

I'm from Scotland Yard's murder squad. I want answers to Tod's death. However, Sergeant Steve Miller is seconded to my team because we are aware that offences of a sexual nature might form part of this case. It will be his report on those crimes which on presentation to the CPS will help become the focus of a wider investigation concerning the production and distribution of violent porn films. Some of which we suspect to be actual snuff movies. Anything to add to that, Steve?

Steve

Don't patronize me, Jeanette.

Jeanette

Just reading Sir James here the riot act. Oops. I forgot he is your brotherhood friend.

Steve

No law against that!

Jeanette

I expect you to perform to the best of your abilities to ensure the law of this land is upheld.

Sir James

If part of that process is to destroy my career, business and most of all my reputation, then I feel I must warn you now chief inspector. You are a women living in a man's world. The people that hold the real power are men. Your presence here is a token nod to appease the women's rights campaigners. A Metropolitan whore metaphorically speaking. To be used for a specific purpose. That is to be a pawn in a larger game of chess. Sometimes crimes are presented to the police that due to their sensitivity and political implications, are deemed by your male superiors as loss leaders. In other words, there are no winners or losers – just victims. There is nothing to be gained from a prosecution. So a decision is made, to allocate these impossible cases to those within the force whose careers can be sacrificed. Namely those ho' bitches that were given rank. In other words, you chief inspector! A general will always look upon his sub-ordinates as collateral to be forfeited if the need arises.

Jeanette

And Tod? Was he surplus to 'requirements'?

Sir James

Why do you think women aren't allowed to join the Freemasons? You're neither strong enough nor well connected enough to cherry pick your cases. Now with that in mind I will answer certain questions. But I will only go so far without legal representation here. Far be it from me to be seen as preventing you from doing your job! Just remember that whatever I tell you will not mean you will get me in court to repeat it. So make no notes, and no recordings.

Sonia

In other words see no evil, speak no evil, hear no evil.

Sir James

Just like Tod – a necessary evil.

Jeanette

So tell us how and when you met Tod.

Sir James

I first met John Sweeney who I later knew as Tod back in 1980. I was the patron of the association of boy's clubs. My company was sponsoring an international boxing competition at the Albert Hall in London. England verses Italy. Tod was a welterweight of great potential. A couple of professional promoters had come to see him, specifically to try to sign him up to the paid ranks. England were dead level at the close of the evening, and Tod's bout was top of the bill. Before the fight I had been approached by Richie Wenton, who was a journalist for *Boxing Weekly* then. He took me to one side and asked me, in his words, did I want to make a shed load of money? Forever the businessman, I agreed. He then pointed to a table full of very smartly dressed men whom I later found out were from Rome. Richie said they had put down a vast some of money on their Italian boxer to beat Tod, and that he knew I could afford to bet against them by backing Tod to win. So I went to the changing rooms and asked Tod's trainer if I could have a quiet word with him. He was skipping in a tracksuit sweating buckets, as he had already failed to make the weight. I was struck by his energy and enthusiasm. I told him about the table of Italians who were betting heavily that he would loose the fight. I asked him, should I bet against them and back him to win? He started to laugh which disturbed me in its tone. He said if Richie Wenton was to go and tell the men to double their bet, then he would encourage me to match the belief that they had in their boy, by placing a bet on him winning. But there was a catch. If he lost by points, I would pay him a grand for trying his best. If he won by points, he would get half my winnings. But if he knocked the guy out, he would bag the whole lot, plus a bottle of champagne for each of his trainers.

Gary

So don't keep us in suspense. What happened?

Sir James

Unbeknown to anyone Tod had taken his opponent to one side and told them about the men from Rome and that not only that they were Mafia. Told him that if he didn't win the bout they'd lose a fortune in bets the end result being they'd take him down a back alley and shoot him. So, Tod tells him to breath slowly in the first round, making sure his mouth was wide open and to pretend he was having difficulty breathing. Then, embracing his opponent, and praying for his soon to be departed soul, Tod walks off saying "no pressure then". The poor lad who was from Sicily as it happened was terrified and by the time he entered the ring he was a walking wreck. This wasn't helped by Tod pulling his glove across his own throat in a gesture that couldn't be misinterpreted. Tod comes storming out for the first and lets go with a solid right uppercut. We could actually hear the poor Italian's jaw go crack! Tod had told me you could only break someone's jaw when their mouth was open, as it was a hinge joint. There was total silence in the hall, until the doctor brought the distressed lad round with a large dose of smelling salts. Tod insisted on giving the Italian half his winnings. He could be a right soft git at times

Sonia

You sure it wasn't poppers?

Sir James

Don't interrupt me! Now where was I?

Sonia

(smiling innocently) Sniffing smelling salts by any chance?

Sir James

Ah yes, Tod was a winner in more ways than one that night. I put him up at the Café Royal as a treat and the rest is history.

Sonia

So Tod already knew Wenton by then?

Sir James

He had said Wenton was his first client before going on to Piccadilly, at Wenton's suggestion.

Jeanette

So you admit you were a client of Tod's?

Sir James

I admit boxing is a sport I am very attracted to. I went to public school of course. Slept in a large dorm full of spotty boys who masturbated so much they had calluses on their hands. Late at night our housemaster used to come in and choose a new plaything for his evening entertainment. If you were lucky it would entail a mutual fondle under the bed clothes. If you unlucky and came from a particularly privileged background like myself then he would invite two other housemasters to his digs. You were then passed from one to another for them to rape, abuse, humiliate. The more they drank the worse the assaults got. He would strap me until I bled with his Lochgelly tawse. Then I would be made to be a human sandwich for his fellow deviants. That meant I represented the soft warm filling. Later in life when I did national service, I became the master, with the power and opportunity to seek my revenge. Which I did, in spades. You would be surprised what young men will do to facilitate a weekend pass so they could visit their girl friends for sex of the normal variety. I go both ways in my taste, officer.

Jeanette

You're what's known as a "switch" in S&M circles?

Sir James

No comment.

Gary

Does boxing come into your passion for controlled violence, sir?

Sir James

Boxing represents one of the few outlets for men like Tod. Working class background. Tough loner types who have something to prove – to themselves and society in general. They might have been abused, bullied or assaulted in younger life. They need a challenge that will set them apart from others. A steely will to overcome fear and to conquer their demons. They have a chip on their shoulder that can hide a multitude of aggression and anger issues. Also a willingness to train their bodies and discipline their minds to the limit, and beyond. Nurturing their newly found fighting talent, in one of the often run down sweat houses that provided a refuge for these gym dogs. A controlled rage, that they will freely exhibit for three minute rounds of mayhem. Only to then embrace each other afterwards in acts of mutual respect. Tod knew the value of this new found asset. Especially with the likes of me. Public schoolboys were fair game to be exploited in his eyes. His instinct to pick up on the smallest detail of what toffs like me, fantasized about was really uncanny. He had studied human behavior bent over large books in libraries. Reading up on historic dictators as well as volumes on psychology, physical anatomy, war books by the dozen specializing in the atrocities committed by the Nazis's at horror holes such as Auschwitz and Treblinka. Places he visited later in life so he could breathe in the smell of fear. To absorb how far man could go in his ghastly games of torture, pain and death. Japanese prison camps where the guards would throw three thousand starving men together and watch who survived the best after a week. The ten per cent that emerged in one piece were deemed to be the dominants who were then taken out and shot, the rest being passive then required little security. And then he would just sit quietly in public places where crowds gathered. Train stations, hotel foyers, doctor's surgeries, churches, jobcenters – anywhere he could study how men and women behaved in different environments and stressful situations. He was putting in these silent lonely hours of observation and research with one goal in mind. To be the master everyone who had been brought up like me would want to serve. Tod was totally unpredictable, and I don't know if that was a deliberate tactic, he employed to keep us 'critters on our toes', as he would often remind us. Or that his mood swings were natural exhibitions of his own inner turmoil. I think it was a com-bination of both. Because it represented the last bit of the secret ingredient, that made him stand head and shoulders above the rest. For him to be able to switch, from being a truly horrible demon one minute and then literally change his whole demeanor with the flick of an eye, was for people like myself, like watching a God, who we would accept anything thrown at us just to be in his presence. Do you understand now how intoxicating the attraction Tod would have to a worth-less shit like me, officer? (*smiling at Sonia*)

Sonia

Tod was your release valve – from your success and from your own guilt of abusing people. He made you feel worthless and humbled you with the use of humiliation and pain. You said to yourself: *if Tod can live with his demons then so can I*. He was your Devil-like fuck-buddy, except it was your mind he was penetrating not your body. Isn't that right, Sir James?

Sir James

You really are a rare breed, my dear!

Sonia

What's that, sir?

Sir James

(*smiling*) A bitch with a brain!

Sonia

Coming from you I'll take that as a compliment. You do know sarcasm is the lowest form of wit?

Sir James

I really don't care how you take it. Just take it! Oh and for your information – sarcasm is the highest form of intelligence.

Jeanette

Did you murder your God Tod by suffocating him and then putting his corpse in a hold all as a gesture of your anger, and as a reaction to Tod going public with his life, in the form of a film and a book? A book you bought out to stop the public, from learning about the hypocrisy you spout out, as a so-called respectable citizen?

Sir James

(Shouting angrily and delivered loud and fast) Detective Chief Inspector. Have you the audacity to insinuate that I should tolerate such diabolical insults from a person of your theology? If so your presumptions are precisely incorrect. *(Gathers his composure)*. I think it's time to bring this tea party to a close. My wife is due back any moment. I will get Gregory to show you the way.

Jeanette

Oh I know the way alright, Sir James. Forward, onward and upwards to the CPS, who in turn will decide whether to take your case to the Old Bailey. Like the old saying goes: see you in court. Thanks for your hospitality but I think I'll go home and puke now.

Sir James

There is just one more thing you need to know about . . .

Jeanette

What is that, Sir James ?

Sir James

I have announced via your press office, that I am putting up a £20,000 reward specifically for anyone who was with Tod in his flat at the time of his death to come forward for a DNA test. I believe you have E-fits of a couple seen leaving the apartment block that were composed from CCTV images you have. They must be your most likely suspects?. The money is specifically targeted at them. So they can be eliminated from the murder squad's enquires.

Jeanette

First, as you can imagine there is a beurocractic process to be completed. Any reward has to be authorized by a commander within the police service. The provenance of any monies must be reviewed. Additionally, there are a lot of legal considerations to be given to the wording of any offer. The E-fit couple are people of interest, not suspects. And above all else, you are now my chief suspect, so no Commander within the force will touch your deflection offer with a barge pole!

Sir James

Detective Chief Superintendent George Frankish has already done so. (*Glances at watch*) He just over-saw a press conference outside Scotland Yard. In boxing terms, I have just counter-punched you.

Jeanette

Then I will come back in the next round, looking to knock you out.

They EXIT. Steve offers Sir James his hand.

Jeanette

No need for funny handshakes, Steve. Save it for your next lodge meeting

Sir James *(dials a number on his mobile)*

They have just left, how did it go? (*Pause*) Excellent see you later at the club. Looks like I owe you a large one.

End of Scene One

Act Two

Scene Two

Hendon Murder Squad office. The team are busy either on the phone or reviewing evidence when Trevor ENTERS. He looks ragged and depressed.

Jeanette

Trevor, this is a pleasant surprise. Have a seat. Looks like you've been burning the candle at both ends. Coffee? Gary – you be mum. Fetch Trevor a large black with none, will you?

Gary

You got it, boss. Morning, Trev. How are you?

Trevor gives a half smile/half grimace in reply.

Trevor

I should thank-you, Jeanette. You've always treated me with dignity and respect over the years.

Jeanette

You know me Trevor, I get that butterfly in my stomach whenever we meet. I have to be honest and say it's purely selfish – I do hope you've brought me something new to chew on regarding the Tod case. God knows we need a break right now.

Gary places the coffee on the desk in front of Trevor.

Trevor

Thanks, Gary. (*Sips coffee*) Jeanette – I've got to be honest with you.

Jeanette

I thought you always were?

Trevor

Well yes, and I have, but regarding Tod – I'm in a difficult position. I've contacted by one of your commanders, whom I'm not allowed to name.

Jeanette

Do you want to talk in private?

Trevor

In any other circumstances I'd say yes, but not in this case. I am not prepared to compromise your position Jeanette or our relationship. I have the utmost respect for you – and that goes for the rest of your team.

Jeanette

If this is going to be painful, I'd rather you make it short and sharp.

Trevor

A Tod delivery then. I'll get straight to the point. I've been told this has come from much higher up than a mere commander. Even the Home Office has stuck their oar in. Basically I've been instructed to bring in a open verdict or death by misadventure on Tod.

Sonia

Trevor – whatever we think of Tod's role in life, the fact remains he was murdered and that is what Jeanette intends to prove.

Jeanette

You're not going to do a smear job on Tod, are you, Trevor? Another man that betrays him, even in death?

Sonia

Look, Trevor. Why don't you consider bringing in a narrative verdict? That way you are at least acknowledging Tod was killed by a person or persons, as yet unknown. It leaves the option open then for the murder squad to continue to pursue fresh lines of enquiry in order to bring it to court at some later date.

Jeanette

Trevor, we need to send out a clear message of intent. I want my squad to use this case to change long-held attitudes of contempt for people who for whatever reason make an informed choice to take part in S&M activities however dangerous or bizarre they may appear.

Trevor

Although this type of verdict was only introduced in 2004, I'd agree it would prove the most viable option here. But I can't emphasise enough that this case is now being managed by more powerful hands than mine. And they want the case to quietly slip into obscurity with the minimum of fuss.

Jeanette

I cannot believe a man who I have respected so much over the years, is prepared to sell himself out to others?

Sonia

Isn't that exactly what Tod did all this life? And yet we all seem to pimp ourselves out one way or another.

Trevor

We're all facing cut-backs, in budget and manpower resources.

Jeanette

Yours isn't the only department that's suffered, Trevor. What you're really saying, is that the Masonic connections that Tod so freely cultivated over the years, the very people he used to shield himself with, are the ones now intent on covering this up. Now who has the motivation – and the means – to do that?

Trevor

You know very well I can't answer that directly in front of witnesses. Don't you think I don't appreciate that or how painful it makes this? But if I don't bring in either one of those verdicts and ensure the inquest is fast-tracked then bang goes my pension. I only have another 12 months to go. Not only that, my department will be merged with another one and I'll be replaced with a younger and cheaper alternative.

Jeanette

They can't do that! You haven't put in all these years of hard graft only for them to turn round and kick you in the teeth. Fight it Trevor. Try getting your union involved.

Trevor

That'll take years. this has come at the wrong time for me, Jeanette. My wife Mary is half the woman she used to be. Regular bouts of chemo have knocked her will to live. I've realized too late that I've given this bloody job more of myself, than I have ever given her. I have to try making her life as comfortable as I can. But it's too little too late. You know what? Now I know she is dying, I have only just started to appreciate her beauty. She has been my eternal rock. Supporting me without question. All those bloody middle of the night calls to attend Death at his sharpest edge. Washing my clothes that stank of some poor victims puke, shit and the one smell she hated, but recognized most of all, fear. My first murder I attended was of a young woman, a single parent struggling in a lonely spiral of debt, soap opera's and poor diet, but who still had fantasies of being a model. She didn't have the funds, or the opportunity to socialize, so she started an affair with her married milkman. He makes her all the promises he can, knowing that with two kids at home and a crippling mortgage to pay, that he can't make any of this young girl's dreams come true. She finds out about his other life by chance. In her anger and distress she threatens to tell his wife. Probably said it in the heat of the moment; you know when you feel raw and hurt, and want revenge to take away your pain of rejection, as quickly as possible. A knee jerk reaction we are all capable of. But he calmly picked up a kitchen knife and went after her from room to room. Such was his pent up frustration he smashed each door down with his bare hands. All the while she was pleading for mercy, even peeing her knickers, then vomiting over the floor, sweating all over her young still lithe body, and just before he cut her throat from ear to ear. She couldn't control her bowels any longer, and defecated where she stood, looking right up at the peeling ceiling, in her final act of indignity. The task of examining her lifeless body was made all the much harder by the fact that both her eyes had tears held in them still. I absorbed her last moments when she was alone and frightened. Little did I realize that I was literally impregnating her bodily smells into my clothes. My dear Mary washed by them by hand diligently, without complaint that same night. Animal instinct told her something, but she didn't know what it was. That night she asked me to hold her close for a moment. A rare request, for I thought of her as such a strong robust character. She whispered in my ear. "Why do I smell almonds on your clothes? Amongst all the vile stains of death?" For a moment I was lost for words. For the murdered woman's mother had visited her daughter, an hour before her death. She had stopped for a cup of tea, and had brought her only child a small treat to try cheering her up, one that as a small girl she had always enjoyed. A cherry bake well cake, it was her last bit of joy, before her sad lonely life was snubbed out in the most brutal of fashion. Well, it's time I remembered that young life wasn't wasted. For it's her death above all the hundreds of others that has reminded me probably too late – where my priorities should be. I'm sorry, but Mary needs me to hold her again, I just hope we have enough time to renew our love for each other. Maybe one day the truth about Tod's death will be allowed to surface, but I won't be around to hear it. Goodbye, Jeanette. And thank you for all your respect and professionalism over many dark episodes.

Jeanette

Trevor – really I am at a loss for words.

Trevor

Don't waste your sentiments on me. Think of yourself and your career. But most of all, your life. Tod survived for a long time in his world of danger. His luck ran out. Don't let the same happen to you Jeanette. Goodbye everyone, and God bless you all.

Trevor shakes Jeanette's hand, turns and EXITS with a pained expression of regret.

Steve

Well, case closed. Tod gets filed under historic cases. Job done. Let's go have a beer.

Sonia

I need to get something off my chest, Steve! *(She positions herself right in his face)*

Steve

I thought being a lesbo you didn't wear a bra. You know – easy access and all that. Don't they call Irish lesbians gay licks?

Sonia slaps his face, hard.

Sonia

Why don't you hit me back – that is if you think you're man enough.

Steve spits in her face instead.

Steve

Fucking bitch! (*Storms off-stage*) You'll pay for that bitch!

Sonia

(shouting after him) Believe me – it's a price worth paying. Tod's taught me a few things – none of them sexual, I might add. Earn more, give generously, consume less, hoard nothing and celebrate life.

Jeanette

(*Gently helps wipe Steve's phlegm off her face*) That's it! I'm filing a complaint on him first thing in the morning.

Sonia

Please don't. I'm fine and a bit of gob isn't going to give me wrinkles. Besides, it's far better than a black eye.

Gary

I'm sorry Jeanette but if you don't, I will. I've never liked the guy anyway.

Jeanette

Thanks, Gary. It'll probably look better coming from a man anyway. I think I have to play a waiting game with this case. Maybe one day someone will suddenly feel compelled to tell the truth.

Sonia

You mean Sir James Gilfroy?

Jeanette

Well, he is our prime suspect and I know the ripples that are spreading across the network of powerful people associated with Tod will in time create enough paranoia to make him consider his own part he played in Tod's death. He's confronting his own mortality, like we will all have to one day. He may also realize that being a control freak it may be better for him to give his own version of what happened rather than those covert tapes which is how he would be remembered. In the meantime, we'll just have to keep the case open and wait and see. Patience might be the only virtue we have left. Tomorrow we have a funeral to attend. I for one am not looking forward to it.

Sonia

I hate bone yards but the smell of crematoriums is even worse. Reminds me of bad barbecues I've been too.

Gary

Tod is being slotted into a small corner of the church he and Gwen attended. They're going to place her ashes in the same coffin, which I think is a nice touch.

Jeanette

Looks like Tod and Gwen get to party one more time after all.

End of Scene Two

Act Two

Scene Three

Tod *(offstage, singing)*

Above all powers
Above all Kings
Above all nature
And all created things
Above all wisdom
And all the ways of man
You were here before the world began.
Above all kingdoms
Above all thrones
Above all wonders the world has ever known
Above all wealth
And treasures of the earth
There's no way to measure what your worth
Crucified laid behind a stone
You live to die
Rejected and alone
Like a rose
Trampled to the ground
You took the fall
And thought of me
Above all

End of Scene Three

Act Two

Scene Four

A small church. Inside, waiting are the murder squad. DCI Jackie Somber is dressed in her full uniform as a sign of respect. A well-dressed young man enters the church quietly, and sits towards the back, followed closely by Sir James Gilfroy, in full military uniform, who sits on the opposite side. The coffin is shouldered in to the church by three undertakers. Father Declan O'Grady waits at the altar. The coffin is placed on a plinth and a pair of boxing gloves are placed on top along with Tod's leather peaked hat.

Declan

(Soft Irish accent) Top of the morning, ladies and gentlemen. Firstly I want to thank you on Tod's behalf for coming here today, for I know he would have really appreciated it. Like the good man himself, today's service will be a step away from the norm. I got to know Tod very well in the last 18 months or so of his life. He first came to this church with his good friend Gwen, who he fondly referred to as his "bitch with the itch." They never revealed quite what it meant but I was assured it was said in good humour and more important wasn't contagious! *(Looking up)* Thank God for small mercies! The first few services he attended, he exhibited a quite and reserved manner, deeply respectful of his surroundings and was often lost in thought. With the help and encouragement of Gwen he started to let down his natural defensive barriers and opened his heart unreservedly to Jesus Christ, his Saviour. There were many tears shed by Tod during this painful conversion to Christ. Gwen had tactfully warned me that Tod was a man who had led a somewhat colourful life but was now surrounded by darkness. But she assured me that he had become her guiding angel in her most desperate time of need. She described him as her 'dark knight who rode a white stallion'. Speaking of gifts, I am going to embarrass our Tod now and thank him from the whole church for his very generous donation, for God loves a happy giver. It's currently pouring with rain outside and but for Tod's mindful intervention, it would also be raining inside. It was Tod who paid for a new roof, for this, his adopted home of worship. This was a substantial investment, that we would never have been able to raise ourselves. *(He turns to the coffin)* Thank you, Tod; and God bless you. *(To congregation)* I thoroughly enjoyed my days with Tod, probably for all the wrong selfish reasons. He reminded me of myself growing up in Cork, a right young renegade I was, that is until I gave my

life to the work of God. You see I thought I knew God, after four years spent at theological college and three years here, I felt arrogant in my knowledge of the scriptures and could recite most things without even referring to the Bible. But that doesn't make you aware of God's strength and spirit. God wanted talk to become action. I saw that work in Tod before my very eyes. A conversion is never an easy process. You have to go right into your soul and pull out all the mess of days spent sinning, and Tod had more than most. 'Love the sinner, not the sin'. I must just do one thing before I ask a friend of Tod's to come forward and speak. *(He reaches across to the coffin where Tod's peak leather hat sits. He tries it on but it doesn't fit. Turning to the congregation he smiles)* Praise the Lord! Just as I thought, but Tod always said if the cap fits, wear it, fortunately for me it doesn't! *(He then gestures to the young smartly dressed man at the back to come forward and says)* Would you like to come up now my friend?

The young man walks to the front. Declan puts his arm around his shoulders.

Declan

Before we hear this young man speak, Tod wanted you to share a glass of his favourite fizz.

Declan retrieves a tray of champagne glasses and passes them out to the congregation. He raises his glass in a toast.

Declan

As Tod used to say: 'A bit of Fizz will do the biz".

Declan stands back to allow the young man to speak.

Gavin

Thank-you, father. *(He sips the drink, coughs, looks to the congregation)* Ladies and Gentlemen, please bear with me. I've never spoken in public like this before. *(He pauses, then starts crying. Father Declan steps forward and puts his arms round him. Gavin's crying has become uncontrollable now.)*

Declan

You remember the Footprints story Tod told you, don't you? "One night I dreamt I was walking along the beach with the Lord, many scenes from my life flashed across the sky. In each scene I noticed footprints in the sand, sometimes there were two sets of prints but other times there were just one set. This bothered me because I noticed that during the long periods of my life when I was suffering from anguish, sorrow or defeat, I could only see one set of footprints. So I said to the Lord, "You promised me Lord, if I followed you, you would always walk with me. But I noticed during the trying periods of my life, there had only been one set of prints in the sand. Why when I needed you most, you have not been there for me?" The Lord replied, "The times when you have only seen one set of footprints, it was then that I carried you."

Gavin stops crying and regains his composure.

Gavin

Thank you, father. I needed that *(He looks back to the congregation, breathing deeply and slowly.)* Thank you for your patience *(turning to the coffin)* Sorry Tod. I'm proud to tell you my name. It's Gavin Mulvey. For a great number of years I could never bring myself to reveal my true identity for I had abandoned my mum, Gwen, and I couldn't understand why. I just knew I had become very angry, confused and highly embarrassed by my mother's seemingly single-minded mission of embracing her former life as a high class prostitute, and using her life experience to help others understand the myths and certain misconceptions as to why some people choose to pursue such a career. I had shut her firmly out of my life and lived incognito under a false name. To everyone I met I told the same story – I had been abandoned. This of course was a lie but it served a purpose for me to put on a façade. Then one day a smartly dressed man knocked on my door. He gave me an envelope and said he was a private detective and that the man who had hired him would urge me to accept the enclosed invitation. He left and I quickly opened the envelope to reveal its contents. I'd like to read it to you.

> "My dear Gavin, you don't know me yet, but I want to invite you to London. Please find enclosed your first class train ticket. On arrival you will be met by a chauffeur bearing your name on a placard. He will drive you to The Ritz. There you will find me, quietly reading an incredible book. It's helped me through some scary times. It's called the Bible. Gavin, I know your heart hurts and for once, I want to take away pain, no pain, no gain buddy. Do not suffer anymore, Gavin, for after every ending, there is a new beginning. Of course Gavin, you could refuse to make this mystery journey of discovery, but seek and ye shall find. But I feel I know you, even though we are yet to meet. Let me embrace you as a new friend, if you don't take the risk you will never know the danger. Trust me Gavin, you will emerge a better man for it. I mean you no harm. God Bless. Tod".

I went of course; he knew I would, a honed instinct. And Tod being Tod of course had an ulterior motive. After two hours of great conversation drinking vintage champagne and sharing our mutual feeling, on confusion and anger, as if we had known each other for many years. Tod suddenly got up, put his hands in the air and said "OK Gavin, this is when I have to jump into the water and feel the depth, and when I touch the bottom, it is only then, I can push up." I hadn't got a clue what he was on about, I thought we were both drunk at that time. He then ran out and a minute later walked back in arms locked around my mother's neck. He was smiling and she was crying, and then I found myself crying, and then Tod was crying. She was saying to Tod "Please Tod, he won't want me!" to which Tod replied, "Nonsense, shut the fuck up and do what you are told for once woman!"

Well. To cut a long story short, I gained my mum, and a charismatic new friend, But more importantly an inner peace. (*He looks at the coffin*) Thank you Tod, for giving me a second lease of life! I truly wish I could have done the same for you. I would like to recite to you this prayer by Mother Teresa, which Tod wrote on the invite he sent me.

People are unreasonable 'illogical and self centered.
Love them anyway.
If you do good people will accuse you of selfish, ulterior motives.
Do good anyway.
If you are successful, you will win false friends and true enemies.
Succeed anyway.
The good you do today will be forgotten tomorrow.
Do good anyway.
Honest and frankness make you vulnerable.
Be honest and frank anyway.
The biggest people with the biggest ideas can be shot down by the
smallest people with the smallest ideas.
Think big anyway.
People favor underdogs but only follow the top dogs.
Fight for the underdog anyway.
What you spend years building up may be destroyed overnight.
Build anyway.
People really need help, but may attack you if you help them.
Help people anyway.
Give the world the best you've got and you'll get kicked in the teeth.
Give the world the best you've got anyway.

(Long silent pause while he looks at the coffin).

Tod you showed me so much in such a short time, I hope and pray ,your tortured soul, finds the peace you never found in life, but which you now, so truly deserve. Goodbye my friend and enjoy the party with my mum.

Crying he slowly returns back to his seat.

Declan

Thank you Gavin, I know that wasn't easy. Tod came across as a tough nut to crack. But beneath that hard exterior lay a soft heart. Which he wore on his sleeve. I loved the manliness of this guy. I say that without embarrassment.

I don't know the details of Tod's career. He was evasive and sometimes unsure with the answer when I asked what he did for a living. He gave me a whole range of job titles. Entertainment officer, personal development manager, physical training instructor, social worker and finally charity worker because he said he had forgone the pursuit of wealth. Maybe he did all of these tasks within one job.

But once I said to him remember Paul's conversation from sinner to saint.

He had ordered people to be flogged to death. He said he would read his Bible that night. The next day he took me to one side and said: 'ask me anything and I will try to give you an honest answer.' So I took a deep breath and asked Tod have you ever done such terrible deeds as Paul had when he was a sinner?
He nearly choked on his lager. For we were talking the "craik" whilst circumnavigating the parish via the local hostelries, like we do in Ireland. For a brief moment he gave me a steely eyed stare. Then slowly his face started to crease up into that cheeky grin of his.

He stood before me my heart was thundering now. Placing his hands either side of my face – (*Declan uses Gary's face to demonstrate*) I felt for one brief moment powerless but secure in his strong hands. Looking me straight in the eyes he said: "My dear Declan, I have spent the last 30 years cultivating what I know now to be a myth. But would you be terribly disappointed if I refuse to spoil peoples misguided perception of me? I would hate to burst their bubble at this stage of my life. What's important is I now have Jesus, and he knows better than anyone my weaknesses. You don't excitedly buy champagne only to drink it warm and flat do you? (*Looking at coffin and placing his hand on the boxing gloves on the top*) Well Tod my dear friend, you were never flat. Cheers, everyone. Have one last toast to Tod before he makes his last journey to a quiet corner of our church yard. Where we will lay him to rest by the old oak tree along with Gwen, his dear friend in life, and now in death. Maybe I should have tied a yellow ribbon around it? It was Tod's wish that only I would see him lowered into the ground. But Tod would like you all to finish the champagne and reflect on your own lives. Hopefully, even if it's only for a short time. To share in a rare moment of reflection, and to talk straight from your hearts. He would urge you to face this confrontation with your own destinies.

Declan nods to the waiting undertakers to quietly remove the coffin which is led out to the last verse of Lynn Anderson singing

Rose Garden. Sir James turns to the coffin and salutes it as it is carried past. Everyone watches and then there is an awkward silence.

Steve

Pheew! Well I don't know about you lot, but I for one need a drink and seems as Tod is paying (*he pours a number of glasses*), is any one of you miserable bastards brave enough to join me?

Jeanette

(*Looking at her colleagues*) Oh come on then – it's what Tod wanted us to do. (*She hands the drinks out taking one for herself*)

Sonia

Well this is a little surreal, but when in Rome. (*She notices Gavin quietly sitting by himself*) Gavin please come and join us.

Gavin makes his way to the front where the squad introduce themselves. Sir James is left standing awkwardly on his own.

Sir James

Of course you don't want me to gatecrash your little party, do you detectives? That's right Gavin – these good people are Scotland Yard's elite murder squad. They are trying to accuse the wrong person of being responsible for Tod's death. To try ruin and destroy a law abiding citizen, linking him to a hideous crime. That person, in fact is myself.

Steve

Sir James, I think you should shut up before you say something in the heat of the moment that you might regret later.

Sir James

I'm not afraid anymore. Maybe like Tod I've become punch drunk. Yes Gavin, according to this Goon squad I am a cold-blooded murderer. Why don't you ask these nice policemen to show you the covert tapes they have of me and Tod? Not that I was aware of them being made, on behalf of a state-funded TV corporation. They used spy cameras, you know. James Bond himself would be proud of the mission they accomplished. But that is a crime against me. Which means the police will have to charge the filmmaker. Richie Wenton was last seen on a one way ride to Golders Green Crematorium. And then if that wasn't enough. I yes, I the victim, had to pay a great deal of money for those nasty tapes to be handed over to my lawyers. But hell hath no fury like a master scorned. The now dearly departed Tod stole the bloody tapes from under everybody's noses. So then I was blackmailed by Tod into paying another fortune for them to be handed over a second time – by Tod your wonderful God-loving new friend. But these highly educated, but poorly rewarded civil servants – note the word servants, Gavin – implied I set Tod up in some bizarre charade, of recreating scenes from a Pierre Palo Pasolini film. Using the filmmaking skills of the now sadly deceased transvestite Richie Wenton. We lured poor helpless Tod into a threesome with a young couple, who were really trained killers working for the Vatican. Yes, that's right isn't it, officers? I used my extensive Masonic connections to bring over from Italy a young male and female hit squad. Who got Tod relaxed and focused on what he did best. Flogging me, tied to the whipping frame. Yes, you will find my blood splattered all over the wood, but I bled on previous visits so you can't definitely pin-point the time. Meanwhile, Mr. and Mrs. Smith kept Tod pumped up in his nether regions. At some point after, alcohol is consumed. The girl is tied to Tod, and they are given poppers to share. Maybe they were so entwined in passionate kissing, Tod suddenly becomes dizzy and that's when in his slumbering last moments, a plastic bag is gently placed over his head. What a way to go for a stud like Tod. It takes just about the same time as a round of boxing for Tod to step of this earth for good. Then to throw off the scent of blackmail, extortion or just plain thieving, I decide to leave the covert tapes, along with a £15,000 red herring. This is a cheap form of deflection on my part. I mean the police can't prove any of this now Richie Wenton has sucked on his last lollipop. The tapes can't be shown on public TV, which is what they were destined for originally. And should my name be leaked to the press to create some sort of scandal then I will sue Detective Chief Inspector Jeanette Somber for slander and breech of privacy. (*He downs the champagne that was given to him earlier by Father Declan at the start of the service*) This cheap champagne just went fucking flat!

Sir James EXITS.

Gary

Don't worry ma'am, there's more than one way to skin a rabbit!

Jeanette

What do you mean?

Gary

Sir James is still our number one suspect. And we still have him dangling by his knackers right now. The film company that bought out Richie Wenton's Pasoloni productions is NCI media. When they agreed to hand over the covert tapes to Sir James's lawyers, they took steps to protect themselves. They made copies, just in case there was any legal ramifications later on. And they retained copyright on those images. They did this as a precaution, in case the tapes ended up in the wrong hands. Which of course, they did. Maybe they knew Tod wouldn't be able to resist such a tempting blackmail proposition. After all, like the Chinese say 'crisis creates opportunity'. This means that should those tapes happen to get lost amongst the other entire Metropolitan police forces crime exhibits and fall into the hands of the press for exploitation, then NCI will sue Sir James for breech of contract. For it was his own lawyers who were responsible in making sure they were given to Sir James to be destroyed. Sir James will then be forced to explain why he was tied to a whipping frame and thrashed until his blood dripped on to the floor. Sir James is calling our bluff. We can if we choose to make him pay for his crimes in a different, but far more effective way if we want to. I mean I get forgetful about where I put things these days. Must be old age creeping up on me.

Jeanette

I know I have to accept we'll never be able to prove without doubt, how Tod died. His undignified end kind of reminded me of a childhood trauma I thought I'd got over. You know, as a teenager I suffered from terrible acne. Because of this I sort of withdrew into myself – made to feel ashamed and embarrassed due to the taunts my peers inflicted on me. Christ – kids can be so cruel. My self-esteem descended into self-loathing and then depression set in. My nan, God bless her, thought I needed something to take me out of myself and gave me a cute white rabbit. Before long I found myself pouring out all my pent-up anger and sadness to this fluffy but loyal friend. Lilly I named her. She provided me with calm, unconditional love and affection without judgement. I needed her as a form of escapism. Slowly my confidence returned and I accepted that nothing is permanent. My spots and rashes healed in time. But just as my new found enthusiasm for life abounded, my rabbit's life imploded into a slow mournful decline of disease and eventually death. But I know better that ever that we all have a purpose however unclear. What we actually achieve may only be felt after we have left this earth.

Gary

I know this may seem a strange think to say, but I was watching my son playing football for his school team the other evening. This is a rare moment of quality one-to-one time I get to have with him these days. Something I feel guilty about all the time. But as I stood and watched him tearing around the field filling me with pride and joy, I was suddenly gripped by a morbid vision. My son is 12, the same age Tod was when one cold night in 1972, a mere boy not a street-wise hustler. He was like my son, returning home from training. Only to be attacked by two animals whose only intention was to consume a young boy's body. A shiver went down my spine, when I think of the unspeakable pain and fear. he went through in those filthy public toilets. Those savage beasts, tearing his sphincter apart, till they scattered their polluted seed. Leaving him recovering his senses, and dressing quickly before the shame and embarrassment would engulf his already frail mind. Who did he cry out for I wonder? His long departed father? His struggling mum? His only help that night came from his own strength of character, to overcome misfortune. As a father looking at his own son, I can honestly say he wouldn't have survived an attack of that magnitude. Then I found my eyes locked on to the club coach's kit bag. It was red like the one Tod took his last breath in. I thought of Tod desperate, alone and frightened for his life. Who did he call for then in his last moment of crisis. His long departed father? His struggling mum? Or the one element of his life, that he had always struggled with. His savior, the lord Jesus Christ. I now question my own values a lot. I don't want to go through life being totally focused on my job. It could all be snatched away at a drop of a hat. Just like Trevor found with his wife's cancer. Then back to reality. My son was shouting "Did you see it, dad? Did you see that beauty of a goal I scored!?" For one split second I thought of lying, so his feelings wouldn't be hurt. But then I thought, that's exactly why my son wouldn't be able to stand on his own two feet like Tod had done so young. "No, I didn't, son. But I am going to take you to a quiet pub, where you and I will have a man-to-man talk, and I will tell you about a fantastic boxer who I wished I'd met when he was alive. Not a world champion but a guy who definitely punched his weight" My son looked at me studying whether to ask for a Mc Donald's instead. But instinct told him not to. I'm thankful to Tod for making me aware of life's frailty. I don't think we will nail the people responsible for Tod's death. They're too rich and powerful. And Tod's lifestyle doesn't exactly win the sympathy vote. But Tod, if you are looking down, then I for one won't forget you

Sonia

I don't know if it's the champagne kicking in, but I would just like to say – oh God this sounds so patronizing: look we are all flawed. Some of us just learn to cope better. Maybe Tod understood himself. Finally accepting he had led a warped life built on myth more than substance. That surreal moment can drive us all off the deep end. I'm beginning to wonder, is it that hard for us as investigators to accept ourselves? We peer into our own deeply held thoughts and it's unsettling. But like the wet paint sign on the door – we can't resist touching it –

Paul

You know there is one significant fact in all this. Choices! We have to make them every day about dozens of different things. But Tod chose to allow himself to be in a position where unscrupulous people took advantage of him. But he played the game back. It was like one big game of chess. And the pieces were made up of money, greed, power, control, pain, servitude, love, hate, vice, compromise, delusion, grandeur, betrayal, murder, suicide, honesty, God. Tod started his career when there wasn't mobile phones, laptops, websites and all the other pieces of today's technology, that helps people connect. Except that deludes people into thinking that what they see on line, is what you get. Tod used to hustle on the 'dilly. He fondly referred it to as the 'meat rack'. But it involved meeting people face-to-face. Real communication skills were developed. You can't read someone's body language on a computer screen. On the street you're out of your comfort zone, and so you make choices on your instinct and your observation. That was Tod's skill. But the world had moved on in 30 years. The punters who had been brought up in an age when gay sex was illegal, let alone S&M activities, had long gone. Of course it went on then behind closed curtains, but it had a kudos about it, and so set Tod apart from the crowd. Sadly for him, that had now all gone mainstream. Boundaries have been pushed back. I wouldn't say it is acceptable in normal society, but the average man and woman are better informed than when Tod started out in 1980. He now found himself alone, without a family to fall back on. Mourning a friend who had finally got him to embrace the lord and who had carried him all through the times of risky exploits. He was bankrupt both financially and morally. I think the self loathing that had engulfed him after being raped had finally consumed him. His personalized coping mechanism of being a master for a living had now abandoned him. Maybe he had an inkling of what was about to happen. And when remembering Gwen's own bravery, in the face of death, he did what has always been suspected in some boxing fights – he swallowed. That is to say he took a fall when he could have carried on. Perhaps being murdered during a pseudo-sexual perversion was the ultimate price Tod was prepared to pay for a sinful life. You see folks, I have the freedom to get it right or wrong. I am not waited down by beurocractic process. But I will continue to study Tod, and in future lectures I give to the next generation of students. I won't shirk way from reciting in full detail, Tod's colorful but tragic life. We can all learn a lesson from a man who started out angry and violent, but who ended up caring and sympathetic. Cheers Tod. (*He drinks his champagne and EXITS)*

Steve

You lot should start working for the Samaritans, have you all gone soft? Tod had broken the law all his life, and yet you all paint him as this romantic rebel without a cause. When I interviewed him regarding the Erskiene murder, he was evasive and cocksure. At one point I upset him about something, and suddenly he leapt over the table and had his hands round my throat. For one short moment in time I was at his mercy and he knew it, that's the bit he got off on. Although I was bigger I felt his strength and I couldn't match it. His rage made him twice the man he was. Then someone walked in on us and he kissed me on the cheek, "Happy birthday, Stevie boy" he said winking for the other person to clearly see. He had compromised me in a blink of an eye. I felt embarrassed and uncomfortable and he was enjoying the moment. I had to let it pass as a bit of light-hearted banter. I suppose I did learn a valuable lesson though apart from never con a con man. And that's the art of getting one over on your opponents. By simply gathering enough information on someone, (*looking at Jeanette and Sonia and smiling*) you then have a type of insurance policy that you can cash in at any time. Either to damage those people, or to gain off them in some way or both. It gives you a sense of strength over those stupid enough to let their guard down long enough for you to strike. A shift in power that can be used at a later date. Tod shaped his whole life like one big fight in the ring. But I have to say those methods seem to work just fine. Tod employed blackmail as a method to control and hurt people. He learnt this subtle form of extortion, from being with his Italian duke Roberto Ferretti, who dangled Tod on a string for 15 years.

Tod had all that time to perfect his craft. But what he hadn't realized that the Duke would leave Tod penniless after his death. Emptying their joint Swiss account was the ultimate betrayal. For it left Tod unable to get answers to where the money had gone. But he shouldn't have had it in the first place. It was a bait put in place, to control this beast of burden so he wouldn't try blackmail the Duke while he was alive. Once Tod had served his purpose he was left stranded. He ended his own life in the fashion he did to make us sit up and investigate his life further – attention seeking to the last. 'There's no such thing as bad publicity' he would often say. He wanted the public to remember him for good or bad reasons.

Either way, he didn't want us to forget him. This is his way of getting back at a society he had been cast out of. The leper has used his disease as a tool to hurt from the grave. You must remember Jeanette and you too Sonia, that someone could have something on you that you are both unaware of. Something small but significant, that can be used against you at any point in the future. A letter, text, email or say a photo.... I mean in this day and age, with computer technology a compromising image can be altered to look very different from the actual scene that was taking place when it was taken. The press can air brush anything to look how they want it. The story along side the photo can be gleaned from a secret source that they are not obliged to name. Just like the police use secret informers.

Let's hope you both have learnt one thing from the Tod case. As far as I concerned there is only one verdict and that's suicide. End of story.

Jeanette

Loathe though I am to admit it Steve, but I'm inclined to agree with you to some degree. People that play with fire should expect to be burnt. I found this note written by Tod, but apparently never sent to Gwen. It reads: Maybe I had something to contribute. It would be meaningless to apologize for what I did, even inappropriate. But I do apologize. I render unto Caesar what is Caesar's. And to God what is God's.

THE END

The following correspondence is between the author and various parties relating to this story.

The original email addresses have been removed and some names have been changed to protect individual privacy.

However, all correspondence is genuine and to preserve their authenticity, these emails are reproduced with grammatical and spelling mistakes intact.

The reader is invited to draw their own conclusions.

Hello Shaun
Hope you're well, in mind and body.
I've had a message from channel 4 saying that someone has made a complaint regarding the title of the film.
I'm not sure if it was you, and if it was, what is troubling you?
Please drop me an email if you need to talk.
Best wishes

Richard Sattin
Principal Television

Hi Tom
Good to see you again. Glad things are going well.
Is it alright if I speak to Lindsey about getting the rushes rolls we talked about?
As I mentioned, I will accompany Shaun and personally see the tapes handed over to the gentleman in question.
Confidentially between you and I, it turns out his name is Sir James Gilfroy. If you want to see his profile it can be found at ....
Not someone to be trifled with!

All the best
Richard

Good to see you too Richard. Yes contacting Lynsey is a good idea. I am in US still, back in UK Monday. I will tell dsp abt them if that is the plan.
All the best,

Tom
Tom Brisley, Creative Director, Darlow Smithson Productions

Hello Tom
Sorry to bother you again. Has there been any progress on this?

Richard Sattin

Hi Richard
Yes there has been progress. We are happy for the tapes to be handed to you and for them to be handed over to Shaun's client's solicitor or destroyed in your presence.
Think Iain was going to follow up on that.
Can you inform Shaun that this is what we are able to do?

Best
Tom

Dear Shaun
There you have it, as received by email.
Name the day and I will make sure they are available to hand. We should meet at your client's solicitor's offices and hand them over.

Richard

Dear Richard.
Thank you for your emails and texts.
Both my client and I are glad that the above matter is close to being resolved.
My client is in touch with his lawyers about your proposal.
They have asked whether they are correct in understanding that the jiffy bag, to which you refer, will contain all the extent tapes relating to your photography of myself and the client?
Am I also correct in understanding that you are not proposing to hand over the other outtakes of which there are a number of hours of still on tape?
Does my client have to be present in the lawyer's office when the tapers are handed over by your good self?
We are looking at the week starting the 29th March as the target week.
The law firm in question is Taylor Wessing, I am sure you will find their London office details on line.
Are there any questions or other considerations that I or my client must consider before then?
We thank you for your discretion and efforts in relation to the matter above.

Regards, Shaun

Thanks Shaun
The client does not have to be present at the lawyer's office. The lawyer simply has to give me a receipt for the tapes saying what will happen to them.
I have all of the master rushes – that's everything that was shot on the day. It therefore includes material that was in the finished programme and all of the outtakes.
Could we please make it the week after Easter?. I can do Weds-Friday.
That's all really. If the lawyer wishes me to make contact with him I'm happy to do so.

Richard

Hi Richard,
Thanks for the clarification.
I will forward this news to my client and his lawyers.
Will look to proceed either thurs 16th April or the fri 17th, will suggest either of these dates to them.
Just to let you know, my client appreciates not having to be there in person.
But on receipt of the tapes, I will take them to him immediately after you have given them to the lawyer and received a receipt for them.
He will be waiting for me in either a restaurant or the pub just at the back of the offices.
I will hand him the tapes and we have agreed he will keep them safely for one year, and then on an agreed date to meet up and destroy them together.
One final question how big is the Jiffy bag as he is worried about storage and safely transporting them on the tube?

Regards, Shaun

Hi Shaun
The bag is not big. It can be put in a supermarket plastic bag.
I thought the whole idea was for the tapes to be destroyed straight away. If the client doesn't want to run the risk of exposure, then why are they being kept for a year?

Richard Sattin

Hi Richard.
Between me and you, he doesn't trust anyone anymore, by holding on them he assures himself that no one can hurt him etc.
I can tell you more once he tells me what his next move is.
I have to act on his orders as you realise he is a powerful man, and I'm a small fish in a big mucky bowl.
Can we talk off record sometime?

Shaun

I'll call you in the next hr Shaun

Richard

Hi Richard.
The date for the hand over of the tapes has now been confirmed by Sir James as Thurs 15th April 3pm.
He has told me today to also inform you, that one of the lawyers, a very nice lady called Justine, will be contacting you by email to make sure they get the wording correct on the receipt for the tapes.
This will be handed over to you from her.
Once I have paid over my monies for the lawyers and Sir James money of which I want a receipt for both.
Justine will then escort me out of the building to a café (I am not told which one yet) where Sir James will be waiting for me to personally hand over the tapes in Justine's presence.
I have told him for the best method of disposal is burning (just like the crucifix in the film) and he will do so on returning to either his London dwelling or his mansion in Norfolk.
I have no doubt he will be eager to complete this whole operation with the min of fuss.
I hope all this meets with everyone's approval.
See you on the 15th.

Regards Shaun

Shaun, Suit's me fine. R

Dear Shaun,
Re: 'Me and my slaves'
We have been advised by Channel 4 that they will not be transmitting the programme again. I can also confirm that whilst the programme is owned and controlled by Darlow Productions we do not have any plans at present to distribute the programme. If that changes we will of course let you know. However, we do wish you the best of luck with the release of your book.

Best Regards,
Pennie Crocker, Head of legal and business affairs

Dear Mr O'Driscoll,
From the outset it was acknowledged that there were potential repercussions to you in revealing your past work as a professional master. The producers have explored the issue of counselling you and they have offered to meet the costs of appropriate counselling advice. The producers have spoken to some of the countries leading councillors who may be appropriate. The producers have spoken with you about the potential legal implications of your admissions on camera about your work and the scenes featuring meetings with clients. You should be made aware they are a prosecutable offence and render you to investigation and potential prosecution

Danny Cohen
Head of Documentaries Channel 4

Dear Sir,
I can confirm that no payment has been made by the producers to Shaun. Channel 4 has very strict rules on payments to contributors and we cannot countenance any such payment given the nature of Shaun's activities. We do however agree to meet the costs of a therapist and I understand that David has made a first recommendation of Ray Woolfe. The film is not blasphemous and this is ultimately a matter for Channel 4.

Danny Cohen

Dear Madam,
The only substantive addition is to brief clips taken from home video footage and a photograph provided by Shaun to the producers last week. The clips and photo feature Shaun and his Italian client. As David explained he was at the time still awaiting some additional material of Shaun and his Italian client. The programme has been slotted into a pre existing short season of late night documentaries focused on the sex industry. The programme title is Me and My Slaves, not Confessions of a whipping boy, which was only a working title.

Yours sincerely,
Andrew Mackenzie Channel 4

Hi Shaun
Thank you for your email and apologies for the previous confusion over my mail address which meant I didn't receive our email on Friday.
I'm sorry that you have not received a reply as yet. I do know, that the lawyer looking after this (Hamish Thomson) has indeed been working on a response but he is not in the office today. I will speak to him first thing tomorrow and hopefully we can get something to your lawyers asap.
Apologies again.

Kind regards
Jane Nuttney, Assistant to Hamish Thomson, Legal and Compliance, Channel 4

Dear Jane
Hopefully you will understand my concern as to why Channel 4 have not responded to my legal team.
3 weeks have passed now, and you said on the phone last week, I was to receive a letter via a Parish Patel.
Maybe you could chase this up as time is running out for me.
It may help channel 4 to know I am heading for bankruptcy in about 6 week.
This might give the impression I won't pursue my claim for damages due to the costs this would generate. However 'if you feed a starving dog it wont bite' would be the reply to that misplaced impression.
I do hope this raises a smile in you if not anything else.
Please let me know if and when the letter to my lawyers will be forthcoming.

Best Regards, Shaun O'Driscoll

Dear Sir

Thank you for your letter dated 18 May 2010 received by us on 1 June 2010. Further to our telephone conversation last week Mr O'Driscoll left several messages with my assistant on Monday confirming that you had consented to us speaking to your client direct. I can confirm that I have now spoken directly to Mr O'Driscoll in an effort to understand properly the nature of his claim and how it relates to Channel 4. In addition, I have also now had the opportunity to meet with representatives of Darlow Smithson Productions.

We must now insist that all future communications in relation to this matter be made between yourselves as Mr O'Driscoll's instructed solicitors and our department as legal advisers to Channel 4.

Although Channel 4 did commission the programme and it was broadcast on 11 April 2006 on Channel 4 as part of the 'Dark side of porn' season we do not accept that the Channel has any liability to Mr O'Driscoll in relation to the claims in your letter or otherwise.

In any event Channel 4's rights are fully reserved in this matter.

Yours sincerely

Hamish Thomson, Lawyer

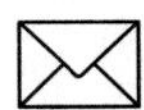

Hi Richey boy.

Last week I made a trip to see Sir James at his London home.

I came away with the covert tapes that were handed over by you in April at the law firm Taylor Wessing.

My attempts to get Channel 4 to compensate me through legal channels have led to them writing to me on the 30th June, with the advice from their lawyer Hamish Thomson to 'contact Darlow Smithson directly'.

But I remember you telling me before you got them to hand over the covert tapes that I was 'going about things in the wrong manner'.

So I would like you to ask Tom Brisley on my behalf:

Will Darlow's now relinquish all rights to the programme Me and My Slaves to myself for £1.

Will they also release to me along with all rights the remainder of all the outtakes to the same programme to myself for £1.

I am sure you will appreciate this proposal would satisfy all concerned.

It doesn't cost Darlows or Channel 4 anything, as the programme is 'dead in the water anyway'.

I would consider myself 'paid in full' and would of course write an undertaken never to bring these matters up again.
My intention is to get control over 'things I said on camera, and certain images I don't want anyone else to see'
If the answer is a resounding no then I can only assume that they have some financial value, as well as some avenue for further explanation.
I haven't gone through a legal channel with this again as yet because it will all be recorded and that could come back to 'bite us'.
Lets clear this ugly matter up once and for all.
Ps. I sent George Michael a copy of my play Damaged Goods.
Got to be better than 'shower time' at Highpoint prison, where's the soap, yes it does.

Shaun

Shaun
Show me the pictures of the tapes themselves.

Richard

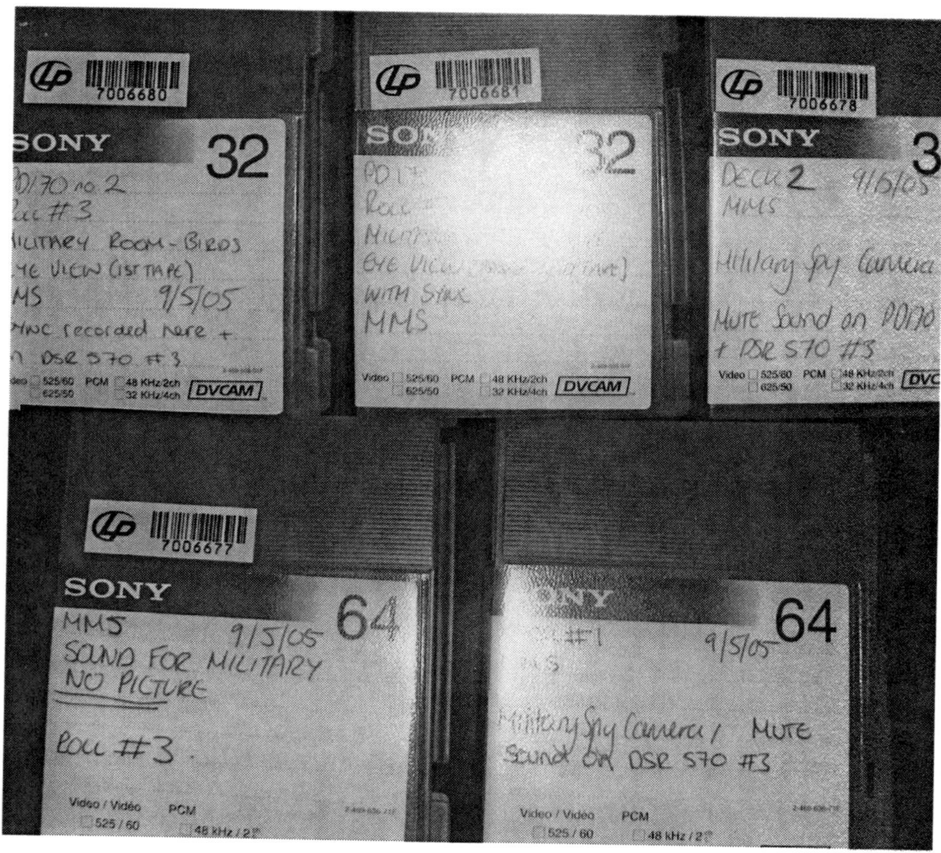

Original Tapes *Me & My Slaves*

Richard,
My life was destroyd by this film long ago.
Where as Channel 4 and Darlows can well afford the collateral damage, for they retain the opportunity to make more profit from the ensuing publicity this case will no doubt throw up.
Maybe you have an interest there as well? We will have to wait and see:
You will have to explain ALL your actions and motives.
Just like I will.

Shaun

Dear Shaun
You asked me to secure the tapes of Sir James Gilfroy because you pleaded poverty and said you needed to return them. For six months I resisted any involvement.
Against my better judgement I asked Darlow to allow them to be returned. They were then destroyed as per the agreement with Sir James' lawyers. We have the papers to confirm they were destroyed.
You then attempted via your solicitor to claim a breach of confidence.
You were advised what the consequences could be for you personally.
There are sections of this and other emails that I am told are tantamount to harassment, extortion and threats. Please understand that I will not tolerate this any more.

Richard

Dear Mr O'Driscoll
To be absolutely clear, all tapes in Darlow Smithson's possession were handed over to Taylor Wessing on the basis of an undertaking from their client to destroy the same. As far as we are aware there are no other copies in existence.

Sincerley,
Julia Pearce

✉

Hi Shaun
Just to acknowledge your email and I have passed you on to Hamish.

Kind regards
Jane Nuttney

✉

Dear Jane
Please could you inform Hamish, that the covert tapes mentioned below in an earlier contact are now going to be presented to the police tomorrow Thursday 20th to be used in a criminal investigation of Richard Sattin, for the criminal act of voyeurism.

Regards,
Shaun

✉

Dear Shaun
I've passed everything on to Hamish for you.

Regards,
Jane

✉

Dear Jane
Could you please get Hamish Thomson to answer this important question. Were all the procedures and codes of conduct as stated in Channel 4's website followed regarding the covert filming taken during the production of Me and My slaves?

Shaun

✉

Hi Shaun
Just to let you know that Prash Naik, controller of Legal and Compliance is now looking into this, so I have copied him into this email.
Regards

Jane

Thanks Shaun – we have the DVD here and I have forwarded your email and attached letter onto Prash

Jane

Dear Prash
Darlow Smithson released the original tapes via Taylor Wessing in 2010, having made copies first. Richard assured me they would not hand over dangerous material without such a precaution which made the whole gesture a hollow one, designed to buy time and deflect my client. I tried to get them to sell me the copyrights to the said tapes, they would not. A clear sign of retention of what they consider to be value. This is also why they insisted in the wording of Richard's receipt for the tapes, that they were to be destroyed.
My client and I would be back to square one then.
Camera 3 at the end of the DVD is I am afraid by far the most damaging images and I have spared Hamish having to view these, they follow my client and I around the room like a hunter with his prey in his gun sight.
If after seeing such graphic material, gathered illegally, by Richard and his crew, who incidentally were being paid out of Channel 4s £150,000 commissioning fee. These tapes were then labelled by Lyndey Neale 'me and my slaves'. Would you be willing to explain in a criminal court why my client and no one else was chosen to be filmed covertly without their knowledge for an ill fated project that lacked thought or cohesion.
Hamish might notice at the end of camera 3 I have changed into a top, clearly written across the front in large font 'Guilty'. Was I trying to convey my inner thoughts to the crew stationed in the room above?
One positive email from Hamish this week, will prevent the police from having these tapes put into their safe but neutral hands.
I will not try to confer Richard or Darlow Smithson in this matter. If channel 4 wish to take control of this situation, they can deal directly with myself.

Shaun

Dear Mr O'Driscoll
For the avoidance of any doubt Darlow Smithson and Richard Sattin have again confirmed that no copies of the tapes referred to as 'Military room tapes' were retained by them. As you are aware all tapes were handed over to Taylor Wessing solicitors, initially at your request, and subsequently at the request of the solicitor's acting on behalf of their client on 15th April 2011. Written confirmation that the tapes had been destroyed by their client was provided by Taylor Wessing on 29th April 2010. If it is true that you obtained the tapes directly from the client as you claim in your email of 4th October 2010 to Richard Sattin, and that some of the rushes that appear on the DVD you sent us come from those tapes, it would appear as though the confirmation that the client provided to Taylor Wessing that he had destroyed all the material.
We do not believe that any offence has been committed under section 67 of the Sexual Offences Act 2003.
As you know my colleague Mr Thomson wrote to your solicitors, Robert Meaton and Co, in June 2010 in response to their letter dated 18th May. In that response he made it clear that any further communications in relation to the matter should be made between your solicitors and Channel 4. We have received no such communication from Robert Meaton & Co to date. Should you wish to consult with solicitors again or at any time in the future we would be prepared to correspond with them.
However we are no longer prepared to engage in any further correspondence or communication with you directly. We would also ask you not to send anymore emails or unsolicited material to us. If you continue to do so this will simply be placed on file, without any acknowledgement, pending any formal claim or police investigation.

Prash Naik
Controller of Legal and Compliance, Channel 4

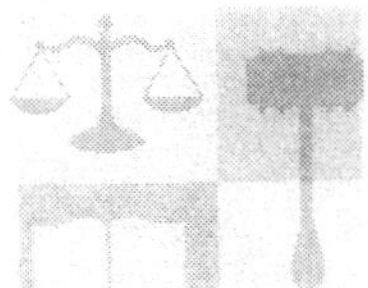

Robert Meaton & Co
Solicitors

Victoria Buildings
4th Floor
1 Princess Street
Manchester
M2 4DF
DX 14424 Manchester 2
Tel: 0845 634 9955
0161 819 5244
Fax: 0161 833 4251
E-mail:
andrewdavies@rmandco.co.uk

Partners:
Robert Meaton LLB Andrew Davies LLB

Our Ref: ANDD/O0008/2/

Your Ref: Jane Mnuttey

18 May 2010

Ms Jane Mnuttey
Channel 4

Dear Sirs,

Re: Our Client: Shaun O'Driscoll
Film: Me and My Slaves

We are instructed to act on behalf of the above named client in relation to the commissioned film "Me and My Slaves".

Our client would like to bring to the attention of Channel 4, a number of issues regarding the Channel 4 commissioned film, which was broadcast on 13th April 2006.

We understand that on the 15th April 2010, at the central London offices of the law firm Taylor Wessing, Richard Sattin, representing Darlow Smithson's Productions, handed over 5 tapes/rushes that were filmed using spy cameras during the making of "Me and My Slaves." This recent development has now caused a significant amount of problems and distress for our client.

Our client informs us that the film was commissioned by Danny Cohen in December 2004. The initial film maker was Principal Films, who did the first set of filming on the 7th May 2005. That same crew on the 9th May 2005 conducted covert filming using spy cameras of our client and his well known client. We understand that Principal Films was subsequently bought by Darlow Smithson Programmes, who then completed the film, bringing in David Barrie as the director.

During the filming, our client agreed to be a party to convert filming, on the strict understanding that his co-operation in the matter would be kept confidential. These latest events have clearly breached the confidentiality agreement, and our client regards this as a breach of his trust and confidence.

Regulated by the Solicitors Regulation Authority
SRA Number: 421152

Dear Jane,
I understand from my client that you have not received a letter from us.
For the avoidance of doubt, please see a further copy.

Regards,
Andrew.

Channel 4
124 Horseferry Road
London
SW1P 2TX

Telephone 020 7396 4444
Textphone 020 7306 8691
channel4.com

Direct Tel 020 7306 8725
Direct Fax 020 7306 8367
hthomson@channel4.co.uk

Robert Meaton & Co
Solicitors
Victoria Buildings
4th Floor
1 Princess Street
Manchester
M2 4DF

30 June 2010

By Fax: 0161 833 4251
Email: andrewdavies@rmandco.co.uk

Your Ref: ANDD/00008/2/

Dear Sirs,

Channel 4: Me and My Slave tx, 11 April 2006 (the 'Programme')
Your Client: Shaun O'Driscoll

Thank you for your letter dated 18 May 2010, received by us on 1 June 2010. Further to our telephone conversation last week Mr O'Driscoll left several messages with my assistant on Monday confirming that you had consented to us speaking to your client direct. I can confirm that I have now spoken directly to Mr O'Driscoll in an effort to understand properly the nature of his claim and how it relates to Channel 4. In addition, I have also now had the opportunity to meet with representatives of Darlow Smithson Productions.

Despite our best intentions that the phone conversation with your client should be helpful and constructive, unfortunately this was not the case. Your client made a number of unsubstantiated claims, some of which directly contradicted the breach of confidentiality allegation outlined in your letter and others that, without further evidence, we are not in a position to respond meaningfully to. We must now insist that all future communications in relation to this matter be made between yourselves as Mr O'Driscoll's instructed solicitors and our department as legal advisers to Channel 4.

Although Channel 4 did commission the programme and it was broadcast on 11 April 2006 on Channel 4 as part of the 'Dark Side of Porn' season we do not accept that the Channel has any liability to Mr O'Driscoll in relation to the claims in your letter or otherwise. In any event and as your client is aware, Channel 4 holds no proprietary rights in the programme or any other material filmed by Darlow Smithson during production. To the extent your client still believes he has an action for breach of confidence or otherwise related to the programme we would suggest you contact Darlow Smithson directly.

In any event Channel 4's rights are fully reserved in this matter.

Yours sincerely

Hamish Thomson
Lawyer

Cc Liam Humphreys, Deputy Head of Factual Entertainment, Channel 4
Julia Pearce, Head of Legal, Darlow Smithson Productions

Robert Meaton & Co | Solicitors

Partners: Robert Meaton LLB, Andrew Davies LLB

Our Ref: ANDD/O0008/2/

Your Ref: Prash Naik

3 November 2011

Mr Prash Naik
Controller of Legal & Compliance
Channel 4
124 Horseferry Road
London
SW1P 2TX

Dear Sirs,

Re: Our Client: Shaun O'Driscoll

We have been instructed by our client Shaun O'Driscoll to liase in the sale of a 71 page play written by our client exclusively for Channel 4.

The title of the play is called TOD "a man for all reasons". This work has not been seen and will not be offered to anyone else. The play centres on and around true events of our client's life including his assistance to Scotland Yard regarding their current investigation into the murder of Gareth Williams.

Within the scenes and dialogue there are a number of references to some secret covert tapes. These tapes are not fictional and do in fact exist. They are entitled military room and all come in DVD format. The reference numbers of the tapes are 504 505 506 507 and 508. Our client states they represent an integral part of the plot of the play's story line. These have been privately held to be sold alongside the play. The scenes shown in these tapes feature our client and a man who is identified within the play under the pseduname Sir James Gilfroy. Our client considers this protection necessary for invasion of privacy issues.

Our client and the person know at Sir James Gilfroy wish to formally acknowledge and except that these tapes are the only ones in existence that contain these particular scenes. Our client is aware of the sensitive and graphic nature of the images on the tapes. With that in mind our client would be receptive to Channel 4 implementing a gagging order regarding this purchase and also any mention of our clients participation in "Me and My Slaves".

Our client wishes to make clear that a proportion of the sale figure will go towards paying off a personal debt made between our client and the man known in the play as Sir James Gilfroy. This this was secured against our client's property address being 15 St Andrews Street, Blackburn, Lancashire, B31 8AE.

Mr O'Driscoll is mindful of the declining health of Sir James and would urge Channel 4 to proceed with the purchase as soon as possible. If for some reason in the future, Channel 4 decides to develop this play in some way, our client would like to assert his rights to be identified as the author of the story line and any credits and financial agreements to reflect this.

Our client hopes this acquisition provides Channel 4 a rare and unique opportunity to acquire first hand insight into a secret world of power, addiction, greed, compulsive urges, control, paranoia, blackmail, violence and death.

We look forward to hearing from you within 7 days.

Yours sincerely,

ROBERT MEATON & CO

Hi Shaun,
I have not had a response or a read receipt acknowledgement yet.

Regards,
Andrew

SPECIALIST CRIME DIRECTORATE

SCD1 - Homicide and Serious Crime Command
Room 2.20 Mayne House
Peel Centre Hendon
Aerodrome Road
Hendon
NW9 5JE

Telephone: 0208 358 0299
Facsimile:
Email: Jacqueline.Sebire@met.police.uk
www.met.police.uk

Your ref:
Our ref: Operation Finlayson

7 February 2011

Mr O'Driscoll

Dear Mr O Driscoll

I am the Senior Investigating Officer responsible for the enquiry into the death of Gareth Williams. I would like to thank you for the coming forward to assist the investigation and the time you spent speaking with DS Christensen.

Your personal experiences and knowledge in this sensitive area provides valuable information which police would normally have difficulty accessing. I appreciate your candid and informed contribution to my investigation. At this time however, I must ask that you refrain from putting yourself to further trouble or expense in respect of this matter.

I must stress that the investigation is on going and I continue to maintain an open mind to all possible explanations for Mr William's death. Should any further evidence or intelligence come to light which indicates a sexual motive for Mr William's death I will of course consider consulting you further.

Yours sincerely,

Jacqueline Sebire
Detective Chief Inspector

Dear Mr O'Driscoll,

I am a Detective Sergeant on the Enquiry Team currently investigating Gareth Williams's death. DS Christopher Quinn has passed your contact details to me. It has not been possible to contact you on your mobile number today ("not possible to connect you to this number").

Given the sensitive nature of the enquiry, I feel the best course of action would be for myself and DC John Bayliss to meet with you Chorley, at a venue convenient to you and, if convenient, would like to do this next Thursday, 25th November. I will of course continue to try and contact you on your mobile number but would be grateful if you would contact me on 07880 995589 when you receive this message. I do understand your frustration at the length of time that has passed since your initial contact and hope this will not deter you from assisting the enquiry.

As I am not permanantly office-based will not be in a position to access emails for much longer this afternoon but am available on the mobile number at any time and look forward to hearing from you. This includes evenings and over the weekend. If you would prefer you can text me and I will call you at a time you suggest as suitable.

Regards

Sonia Christensen
Detective Sergeant
Homicide & Serious Crime Command
Mayne House - Peel Centre
Aerodrome Road
London NW9 5JE

Shaun,
Thank you for your email. There isn't a 'relevant officer' who would look into your complaints against C4 but, as discussed, there are people with knowledge of the subject matter that I will locate and speak to.

Regards,
Sonia.

Shaun,
I have some correspondence for you from the DCI in response to the information you have provided. Please can you provide me with an address for it to be sent to?

Thank you
Sonia

DR FIONA WILCOX

Telephone: 020-7802-4750

Facsimile: 020-7828-2837

Email: coroner@westminster.gov.uk

WESTMINSTER CORONER'S COU

65 HORSEFERRY ROAD

LONDON SW1P 2ED

HER MAJESTY'S CORONER

INNER WEST LONDON

Shaun O'Driscoll

5 July 2011

Dear Mr O'Driscoll

With reference to your letter of 27th June to the Coroner, Dr F J Wilcox, the coroner has asked me to thank you.

The content has been noted and has been placed on file.

Yours sincerely

Miss S Lord
Clerk to HM Coroner
Inner West London

Hello Shaun

In relation to your personal concerns with Channel 4 I believe the best course of action would be report it to your local police.

Such a matter would not necessarily fall within the remit of the Metropolitan Police to deal with due to boundaries.

It may be of great assistance to write things down in a clear and chronological order if you have not done so already.

Alternatively it may be more appropriate to seek independent legal advice and consider civil law options

Regards
Jackie Sebire

Hi Shaun,
Please see the attached letter received today from Channel 4.

Regards,
Andrew

Channel 4
124 Horseferry Road
London
SW1P 2TX

Telephone 020 7396 4444
Textphone 020 7396 8691
channel4.com

Direct Tel: 020 7306 8920
Direct Fax: 020 7306 8367
hthomson@channel4.co.uk

official broadcaster of the London 2012 Paralympic Games

Robert Meaton & Co
Victoria Buildings
4th Floor
1 Princess Street
Manchester
M2 4DF

15 November 2011

Dear Sirs

Re: Your Client: Shaun O'Driscoll

We refer to your letter dated 4 November 2011, received by email 7 November 2011.

Prash Naik is currently away from the office until the 28 November. He will revert to you as soon as possible upon his return.

On a separate point we note your client attempted to contact our department directly twice today. Your client is aware, pursuant to previous email correspondence from Mr Naik, dated 31 October 2011, that we are no longer prepared to engage in any further correspondence or communication with him directly.

We would reiterate Mr Naik's request that your client not phone or send anymore unsolicited material to us. We are only prepared to engage with your client to the extent he contacts us through you as his solicitors.

Yours sincerely

Hamish Thomson
Lawyer
Legal & Compliance

Hi Shaun,
Further to our meeting, I can confirm we are holding the 5 tapes and play in our safe.
I will forward you a draft of the letter shortly.

Regards, Andrew

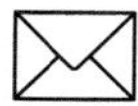

Hi Shaun,
Attached is the letter to channel 4. I will send it out by special delivery today with the enclosures.

Regards,
Andrew

Robert Meaton & Co | Solicitors
Partners: Robert Meaton LLB, Andrew Davies LLB

Our Ref: ANDD/O0008/2/

Your Ref: Prash Naik

24 November 2011

Mr Prash Naik
Controller of Legal & Compliance
Channel 4
124 Horseferry Road
London
SW1P 2TX

Dear Prash,

Re: Our Client: Shaun O'Driscoll

We are writing further to the letter dated 15 November 2011 from Hamish Thomson in your absence.

Our client would firstly like to extend his congratulations regarding the birth of your child and for the letter from Hamish Thomson in your absence.

Mr O'Driscoll would like to confirm that he met with the gentleman referred to in earlier correspondence as Sir James Gilfroy on Friday 18th November 2011, in London. Our client observed the poor state of health of Sir James, and refrained from discussing any of his approaches to Channel 4. However this meeting highlighted the importance of completing this transaction swiftly and as soon as possible.

For these reasons and as a gesture of goodwill, our client has instructed us to release to you the play called "TOD", so that the script can be digested. Our client has also instructed us to send to you tape 508, which is the sound recording for the military room scene shown in the DVD, and which forms part of the purchase package offered. We therefore enclose both the play and tape 508.

Our client hopes this will assist Channel 4 in the acquisition. As stated in our letter dated 4 November 2011, our client would be receptive to Channel 4 implementing a gagging order regarding this purchase and also any mention of our client's participation in "Me and My Slaves".

Mr O'Driscoll is mindful of the declining health of Sir James and would urge Channel 4 to proceed with the purchase as soon as possible. If for some reason in the future, Channel 4 decides to develop this play in some way, our client would like to assert his rights to be identified as the author of the story line and any credits and financial agreements to reflect this.

Our client hopes this acquisition provides Channel 4 a rare and unique opportunity to acquire first hand insight into a secret world of power, addiction, greed, compulsive urges, control, paranoia, blackmail, violence and death.

We look forward to hearing from you within 7 days.

Yours sincerely,

ROBERT MEATON & CO

Dear Andrew
I really think we deserve an answer from channel 4 by now, don't you?
Can you ring to see if one is forthcoming by the end of this week please.

Regards,
Shaun

Hi Shaun,
Sorry I miss your calls, I have a number of meetings today.
I have had no response from channel 4. I agree that we should have had some sort of response by now.
Therefore I will call them tomorrow morning and let you know what they say.

Regards,
Andrew.

Hi Shaun,
I have chased them by telephone, but could not get through to Prash.
However I have just received the attached letter.

Regards,
Andrew

Channel 4
124 Horseferry Road
London
SW1P 2TX

Telephone: 020 7396 4444
Textphone: 020 7396 8691
channel4.com

Direct Tel: 020 7306 8487
Direct Fax: 020 7306 8367
pnaik@channel4.co.uk

london

official broadcaster of the
London 2012 Paralympic Games

Robert Meaton & Co
Victoria Buildings
4th Floor
1 Princess Street
Manchester
M2 4DF

By Email & Post

2 December 2011

Dear Sirs

Re: Your Client: Shaun O'Driscoll

Thank you for your letters of 4th and 24th November 2011.

We are somewhat puzzled by your letters which we must assume are based on instructions provided by your client which are misconceived.

Firstly you appear to suggest that your client has written a play exclusively for Channel 4. For the avoidance of doubt, no play or treatment was ever commissioned or requested from your client and Channel 4 has no interest in acquiring such material. Your firm has provided an unsolicited copy of the transcript called 'TOD' which we are returning unread by post.

Secondly your client appears to suggest that he holds DVD material produced and owned by Darlow Smithson Productions. We understand that these relate to programme rushes that were filmed, but never broadcast for a documentary featuring your client called 'Me and My Slave' broadcast on Channel 4 on 11th April 2006. Your client is well aware that the original material was handed over in its entirety to the solicitors for the man featured in those DVD's by the producers on the basis of an undertaking given by that individual that the material would be destroyed. Written confirmation was provided by those solicitors at the time to that effect and the solicitors have again confirmed more recently that the material was destroyed. We are returning by post the unsolicited dvcam tape marked '508 sound for military room no picture' which was sent to us by your firm which we have not listened to. For the avoidance of doubt Channel4 has no interest in acquiring this material.

Thirdly, your letter appears to suggest that you also act or have spoken with the man featured in those DVD's. We understand that he is represented by Taylor Wessing solicitors and we are unclear what, if any, role he plays in your clients proposals. Conversations your client may or may not have had with him are therefore academic.

Lastly, your client has requested that Channel 4 obtains a gagging order in circumstances which again are not entirely clear. For the avoidance of doubt, we do not intend to obtain any such order.

Finally we have received a large number of emails and calls from your client as have Darlow Smithson, some of which have been threatening in tone. We have previously written to your client indicating that we will no longer correspond with him directly and that all future correspondence must be conducted through his solicitors. We would ask you to remind your client of our position in this matter and would ask him to desist from such phone calls and emails.

Yours sincerely

Prash Naik
Controller of Legal & Compliance

Dear Mr O'Driscoll
This is outside my area of experience and as I have suggested previously I think you would be best served if you sought independent legal advice to provide you with the best options for your ongoing dispute with channel 4

Regards,
Jackie Sebire

Dear Andrew
Lets cut the crap with them. We have to know specifically why they refuse to answer now that they have one of their illegally obtained tapes, back in their possession.
What is their next move?

Regards,
Shaun

Hi Shaun,
Just to confirm I have had the letter and pack back from Channel 4. I have put it in our safe and we will see you at 2pm on Thursday.

Regards,
Andrew

Mr Naik,

Further to our previous email, we can confirim our client Shaun O'Driscoll was interviewed by Lancashire Police on Friday 9th December 2011.

An allegation was made by our client of criminal damage to the covert tape 508, which you returned to us. This was logged with police reference number LC-20111209-0827. However during the questioning, other more serious allegations were made by our client, concerning the production of the Channel 4 programme Me & My Slaves.

The officer deemned it appropriate to now refer these and the intial allegation to the Metropolitan Police. The tape has been retained by the police as evidence. Our client would like to remind you, that you stated in writing to him earlier that "you would fully co-operate and fully explain the circumstances around the filming".

He now feels it futile and inapproprate to continue contact regarding this matter, but he will retain us as his legal representation especially with a view to advice regarding possible court proceedings. Any contact to him should therefore be only through us.

Regards

Andrew
Partner

Me and My Slaves

Receipt

Name: Richard Sattin

Receipt for:
Unused rushes tapes for Military scene in 'Me and My Slaves
Tapes are to be DESTROYED as per agreement via emails

Tape numbers:
All DV Cam

504	Military room birds eye view	9/5/05	(small format)
505	Military room birds eye view	9/5/05	(small format)
506	Military room spy camera (mute)	9/5/05	(large format)
507	Military room spy camera (mute)	9/5/05	(small format)
508	Sound recording (no pic) for Military room	9/5/05	(large format)

5 tapes in total

Issued by: Lynsey Neale

Received: Date:
(sign)

Print Name:

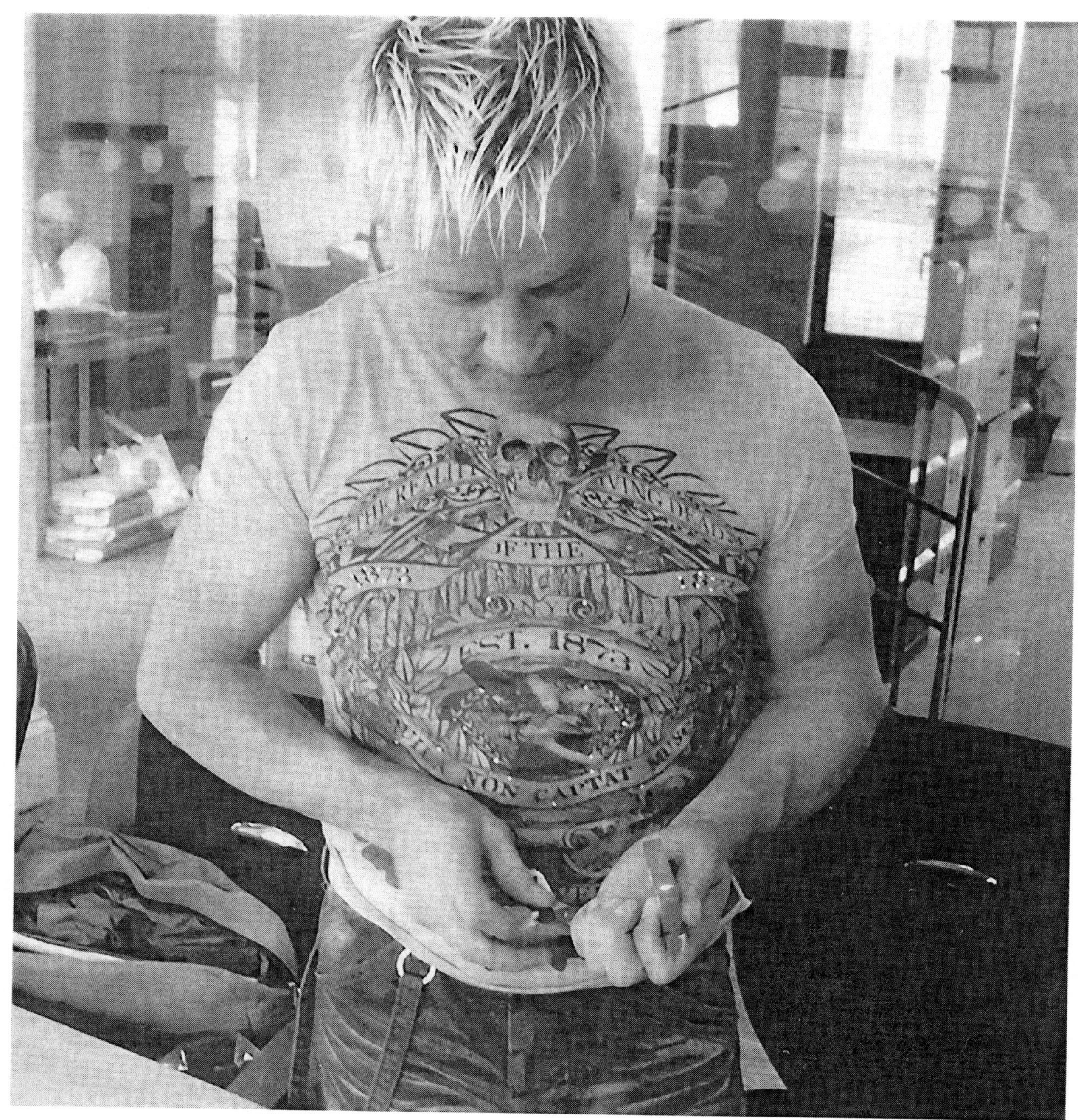

The Author destroying the tapes.

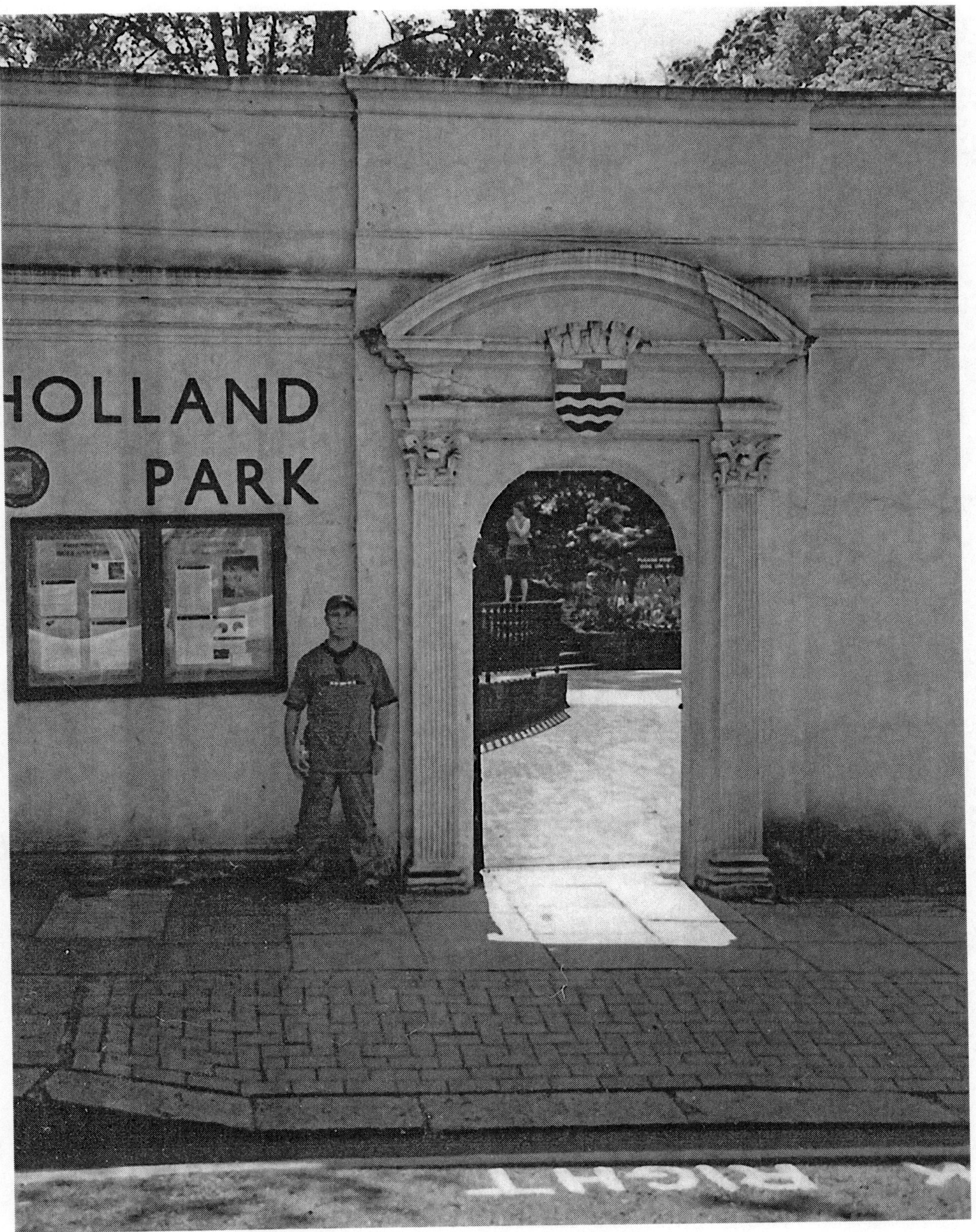

The Real Tod, 2001. Photo taken by Duke Roberto Ferretti.

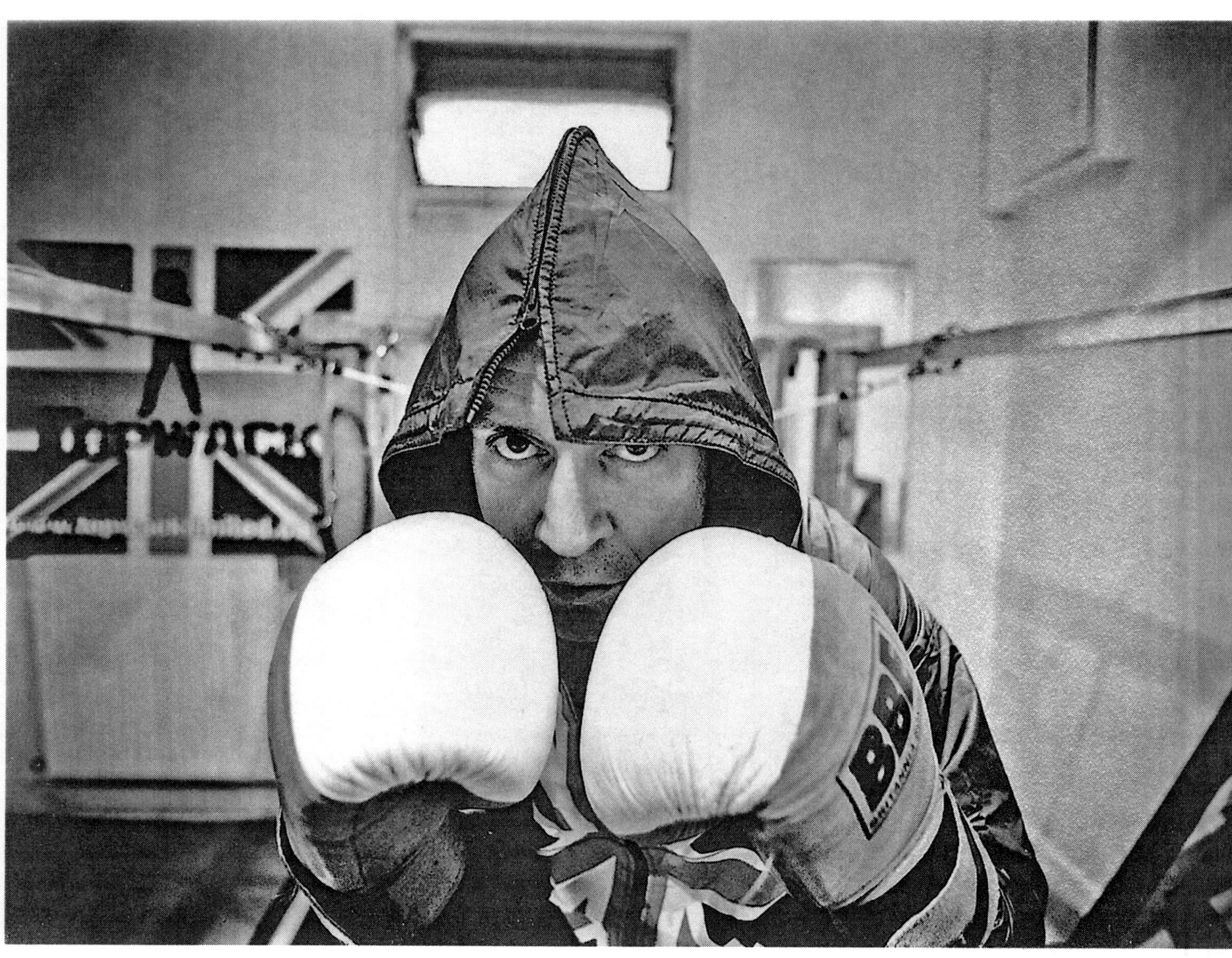

The Author.

Author's Statement

I must confess I originally wrote this play by default. From November 2010 until April 2012, I was assisting Scotland Yard's murder squad with their complex investigation into the murder of MI6 operative, Gareth Williams. As I did not wish to hamper their investigation, I have held back from disclosing details that would damage evidence or hinder a prosecution in court, should they ever arrest anyone. Regarding Gareth's death, I would like to thank DCI Jackie Sebire for her assistance and advice on a number of occasions when I have asked for help.

The play was designed to act as a kind of "Trojan horse" – a tool by which Channel 4 would recognise an error of judgement and then compensate the victim of this mistake, but keep the entire damaging saga well away from public scrutiny. But as Channel 4's intention all along was merely to expose a powerful individual's secret fetish, they firmly refused to accept such a unique solution. Any resulting scandal would be more damaging to a titled individual than a TV corporation seeking further funding.

For the avoidance of doubt. I have used actual emails, legal correspondence and letters to give the reader facts – not fiction. The procedures and protocols highlighting covert filming were written by Channel 4 lawyers to protect Channel 4 legally, should any challenges or legal repercussions arise form this secret method of programme gathering. So we must assume that if Channel 4 followed these very detailed rules then they would have written minutes of those meetings.

When the Metropolitan Police interviewed Prash Naik under caution, regarding the criminal damage done to covert tape 508 he would not produce this evidence when the officer asked for it. Prash did provide a number of photographs of the tape he took personally when he admitted he opened the package it was in. These detailed images showed clearly the tape was undamaged at this point. But when pressed to explain why he took the photographs he gave a "no comment" reply.

Without forensic evidence to assist this enquiry, the charges had to be dropped. I was advised by lawyers that to take Channel 4 to court in a civil action would not be advisable. It would cost upwards of £100,000 and while a charge of voyeurism might convict the filmmaker Richard Sattin, no action could be taken against Channel 4 even though they had commissioned the programme. The covert filming was paid for by them and the resulting production – *Me &*

My Slaves yielded profit. It was Channel 4's legal team who had meetings with Richard Sattin in relation to that covert filming prior to it taking place.

The reader is invited to view Channel 4's Rules of Practice and Procedure for Secret Filming and Recording for Channel 4 Programmes which is available on the Channel 4 website. These appear to have been wilfully and deliberately abandoned during the filming of *Me & My Slaves*. It is therefore the Author's contention that Channel 4 is in violation of their own code of practice.

After much reflection. I also decided not to pursue a charge against Prash Naik of perverting the course of justice. I wanted to move on, but more importantly leave the old and now frail victim known as Sir James Gilfroy free to live out the remainder of his life in peace.

In February 2010, a Channel 4 commissioning editor named Sarah Mulvey took her own life. She had been in conflict with her bosses for some time. This bullying and systematic campaign of grinding down a gifted talent, who dared to challenge the powerful men who controlled Channel 4, left a sensitive young woman, alone and isolated. Perhaps she felt she had nothing left in life worth fighting for. Like Tod in the play, we can only imagine long days of reflection, anger and deep rejection. I hope both Sarah and Gareth Williams are safe in the Lord's arms. May they both Rest in Peace.

Their selective silence speaks volumes about their guilt. But their lawyers' reaction on receipt of one of those damaging tapes says a lot about their arrogance and state of mind.

Perhaps Oscar Wilde described it best:

"I can resist everything except temptation".

About the Author

Shaun O'Driscoll published some of his memoirs in 2008 entitled *Me and My Slaves*. The book was the subject of legal action and withdrawn the same year. His play *Damaged Goods* was later published by Third House Publishing in 2010 and was offered to George Michael. As yet it has not been taken up.

Shaun O'Driscoll is currently immersed in the unlicensed boxing world.

CPSIA information can be obtained at www.ICGtesting.com
Printed in the USA
LVOW111431150213

320336LV00011B/282/P

9 781907 695193